Praise for *The Secret Place: 30 Days of Devotion*

This devotional is rich, relevant, and profound. It's not a check-the-box devotional. Every entry has God's breath in it, and it takes you to a place of relevance, repentance, then healing. It's a must-read!

— *Heather Molchanoff, Deliverance Minister/Entrepreneur*

This devotional is a powerful tool to lead you out of emotional brokenness, a way out and a way how to find deliverance and healing through encountering Jesus.

— *Yolanda Robles, Ministry Director Awaken Church San Diego*

This devotional is one of the greatest gifts you could ever give someone or yourself as it will guide you through a process of healing and restoring the heart. Give yourself permission to experience this journey of transformation and see how God will work in you and through you!

— *Danny Robles, Ministry Director Awaken Church San Diego*

The Secret Place

30 DAYS OF DEVOTION

Dana Piper

FOREWORD BY LEANNE MATTHESIUS

The Secret Place:
30 Days of Devotion
Copyright © 2024 by Dana Piper

All rights reserved. No part of this publication may be reproduced, distributed, or transmitted in any form or by any means, including photocopying, recording, or other electronic or mechanical methods, without the prior written permission of the publisher, except in the case of brief quotations embodied in critical reviews and certain other noncommercial uses permitted by copyright law.

Published by: New Together Inc.

Address all inquiries to: info@newtogetherinc.com

Paperback ISBN: 979-8-9911612-0-6

Scripture quotations marked NLT are taken from the Holy Bible, New Living Translation, copyright © 1996, 2004, 2015 by Tyndale House Foundation. Used by permission of Tyndale House Publishers, Inc., Carol Stream, Illinois 60188. All rights reserved. Scripture quotations marked NIV are taken from THE HOLY BIBLE, NEW INTERNATIONAL VERSION®, NIV® Copyright © 1973, 1978, 1984, 2011 by Biblica, Inc.® Used by permission. All rights reserved worldwide. Scripture quotations marked ESV are taken from The Holy Bible, English Standard Version. ESV® Text Edition: 2016. Copyright © 2001 by Crossway Bibles, a publishing ministry of Good News Publishers. Used by permission. All rights reserved. Scripture taken from the New King James Version®. Copyright © 1982 by Thomas Nelson. Used by permission. All rights reserved. Scripture quotations marked MSG are taken from THE MESSAGE, copyright © 1993, 2002, 2018 by Eugene H. Peterson. Used by permission of NavPress. All rights reserved. Represented by Tyndale House Publishers, Inc. Scripture quotations taken from the Amplified® Bible (AMP), Copyright © 2015 by The Lockman Foundation. Used by permission. lockman.org. Scripture quotations taken from the Amplified® Bible (AMPC), Copyright © 1954, 1958, 1962, 1964, 1965, 1987 by The Lockman Foundation. Used by permission. lockman.org. Scripture quotations marked TPT are from The Passion Translation®. Copyright© 2017, 2018, 2020 by Passion & Fire Ministries, Inc. Used by permission. All rights reserved. ThePassionTranslation.com.

Cover Design and Interior Layout: Fusion Creative Works

Author Photograph: Joel Piper

Dedication

This book is dedicated to my father, Wayne Adams, who was welcomed into the arms of Jesus in April of 2023. You will always be my hero. Thank you for your unconditional love, faithfulness, compassion, and for laying down your life to become the servant of all. My heart is filled with gratitude, knowing you are reaping unlimited eternal rewards. And to my husband, Joel, thank you for choosing me to be your wife, and for loving me in a way I didn't know I needed to be loved until I found yours. Your life truly inspires and challenges me to be a better woman. Thank you for leading our home and family with the heart of a worshiper and the strength of a warrior. I love you with all my heart.

Table of Contents

Foreword	11
Introduction	15
Section 1 - Inner Healing	**19**
Day 1: The Enemy's Greatest Tactic is to Unseat The Soul	23
Day 2: Is Staying The Same More Painful Than The Journey And Commitment It Will Take to Get Well?	25
Day 3: When Pain or Grief Comes, Remember Not to Focus on the Pain or Grief, But The One Who Bore Your Pain and Grief	29
Day 4: Pain is a Journey, Not a Destination. Don't Build an Idol Where You Were Meant to Build an Altar	33
Day 5: The Ultimate Fruit of Healing is Self-Control	37
Section 2 - Deliverance	**41**
Day 1: Your Freedom And Your Transformation Are 100% Your Responsibility	45
Day 2: If You Consume More Than You Produce, You Will Always Live in a Deficit; Beggars Always Borrow	49
Day 3: True Healing Doesn't Happen Until We Surrender Our Disease	53
Day 4: What Sin is Seducing You?	57
Day 5: Warfare is The Key to Possession and Required for Ownership to Change	61

Section 3 - Mind Renewal — 65

Day 1: You Can Be Rid of Your Demons, But Then You Have to Destroy The Lies They Energized — 69

Day 2: What is Not Processed is Repressed — 73

Day 3: Don't Ever Let The Devil Bring Shame And Condemnation Where God is Bringing Awareness — 77

Day 4: God Doesn't Re-Create; He Only Creates. Anytime You Try to Re-create Your Life, You Are Living Under The Wrong Influence — 81

Day 5: Renewing Your Mind Will Transform Your Life, But No One Can Renew Your Mind But You — 85

Section 4 - Prayer — 89

Day 1: As God's Kids, We Don't Have to Pray, "If It's God's Will." We Know Him, So We Pray His Will — 93

Day 2: Dark Seasons Should Never Dim Your Light; They Should Make Your Light Brighter — 97

Day 3: The Purpose of Prayer is Not For God to Take Away Your Problems; The Purpose of Prayer is to Produce The Power to Overcome — 101

Day 4: Sometimes, We Need to Go Without Bread to Get a Word from God. But God Doesn't Want You to Give Up Bread as Much as He Wants You to Give Up Distraction — 105

Day 5: Perhaps Prayers For Breakthrough Are Not About Waiting For God to Move Us as Much as They Are About Praying In Such A Way That Our Prayers Move Him — 109

Section 5 - Fear of the Lord 115

Day 1: Once You See Jesus For Who He Is, You Will Never Live Your Life a Slave to The Substitute 119

Day 2: I Would Rather Use a Wilderness Season as a Training Ground for Future Battles Than Stay Stuck as a Consequence of Complacency 123

Day 3: The Enemy Does Not Want to Steal Your Gift; He Wants to Steal The Oil That You Have Purchased in Secret 129

Day 4: Fear Causes Us to Forfeit Our God-Given Identity and Take On The False Identity of Self-Preservation and Self-Sufficiency 135

Day 5: People Who Fear the Lord Praise; People Who Don't Complain 141

Section 6 - Worship 147

Day 1: God Destroys Your Enemies to The Soundtrack of Your Praise 151

Day 2: The Only Wilderness You Stay in is The One You Complain in; Make The Choice to Rejoice 155

Day 3: If You Want a New Season, You Need to Sing a New Song 159

Day 4: Before You Bring God Your List, Bring Him a Gift 165

Day 5: You Can Praise God For What He Has Done, But Worship is When You See Him Face-to-Face 171

Conclusion 177

Foreword

by Leanne Matthesius

> He who dwells in the secret place of the Most High Shall abide under the shadow of the Almighty. I will say of the Lord, "He is my refuge and my fortress; My God, in Him I will trust."
>
> **Psalms 91:1-2, NKJV**

My life has been forever changed, refined, and challenged by the time I have spent in the secret place. God always wants to speak, but sadly, few are willing to take the time to listen.

The greatest heavenly treasures await those who wait on the Lord! Strategies, answers, wisdom, and supernatural strength belong to those who take the time to spend in the presence of the Lord!

The value of the things found and learned in the secret place is unmatched! Yet few take the time to avail themselves of all God wants to show us!

It is an honor to be asked to write the foreword for Dana Piper's new book, *The Secret Place: 30 Days of Devotion*.

As a beloved pastor, minister, and congregant in our church for many decades, Dana is known by all as a devoted disciple, a faithful prayer warrior, a woman of the Word, and a trusted prophetic voice.

Her latest book is a clarion call to all who long to live in a way that holds absolutely nothing back from God!

Dana's consistent pursuit of God through life's highs and lows has set her apart as a woman who knows how to hear from God in all of life's seasons! Constant and true, the weight of Dana's example has inspired countless others to engage with God in a secret place of their own.

Her involvement in prayer, worship, mission work, and pastoral care has given Dana's writings the well-roundedness of someone who knows what it means to walk with God and walk with people!

Dana shows us through her writing and revelation that the victorious life of an overcomer is available to ALL those who wait on the Lord and are obedient to His leading.

Her teaching on the importance of inner healing, renewing the mind, prayer, and worship will open the hearts and minds of all who want to live as overcomers, a life marked by peace, courage, joy, and victory!

Make no mistake—this is not just another cute devotional! One of the things I admire most about Dana is her ability to go deep into the Word of God and then surface with bold, helpful, timely, and clear words!

The testimonies and revelations within were mined in the places where few people take the time to go.

This book has been forged in a place of deep surrender; revelations walked out with God in the brightest and the darkest seasons of life.

These devotions are life-giving and lifesaving, and the instructions for life are taken straight from her time in the secret place with the author of life!

They are gritty yet gentle, vulnerable but victorious. Dana has taken the complex and made it plain, and I know it will bring life, hope, and courage to all who apply what is written on its pages.

As you read through these daily devotionals, you will be encouraged, strengthened, comforted, and challenged. So, like the young boy Samuel, who became a mighty prophet, let your spirit say, "Speak, Lord, for your servant is listening."

Leanne Matthesius

Lead Pastor Awaken Church San Diego

Introduction

We are witnessing the rise of the unshakeable church. While we continue to experience war, we will see a greater measure of favor if we stand firm.

Hebrews 12:26–27 (TPT) says:

> The earth was rocked at the sound of his voice from the mountain, but now he has promised, "Once and for all I will not only shake the systems of the world, but also the unseen powers in the heavenly realm!" Now this phrase "once and for all" clearly indicates the final removal of things that are shaking, that is, the old order, so only what is unshakable will remain.

The last five years have been the most significant training ground I've ever experienced. During this period, I faced many challenges meant to break me. These battles involved confronting the devil himself, and some even required a lengthy recovery period.

I've had to stand firm in my identity and office as a child of God like never before and exercise my faith to shield the attack on my authority and assignment. And I strongly believe that, both personally and for the church, the past few years have been a training ground for an upcoming war. This war will make the giants of this land bow their knees to the governmental authority of the unshakeable and favored church.

What makes you unshakeable? It is not the battles around you, but the holiness within you. It is this distinction that sets apart the holy from the common.

David writes the description for being unshakeable in Psalms 15:2–5 (TPT):

> They are passionate and wholehearted, always sincere and always speaking the truth—for their hearts are trustworthy. They refuse to slander or insult others; they'll never listen to gossip or rumors, nor would they ever harm a friend with their words. They will despise evil and evil workers while commending the faithful ones who follow after the truth. They make firm commitments and follow through, even at great cost. They never crush others with exploitation and they would never be bought with a bribe against the innocent. Those who do these things will never be shaken; they will stand firm forever.

Despite the chaos in the world, the church hungers to go deeper into the heart of God. Although people may be hungry, they also need more direction and guidance. Discipleship can help them create a roadmap and lead the way.

I believe this book will help. I was awakened by God one day, and He gave me a commission to write a thirty-day devotional titled *The Secret Place: 30 Days of Devotion*.

He said, "Dana, people don't need as many self-help books as they do good devotionals, in the times you are living. I want you to teach people how to live victoriously through building an intimate relationship with me."

Luke depicts this relationship perfectly in Luke 6:47–49 (ESV):

> Everyone who comes to me and hears my words and does them, I will show you what he is like: he is like a man building a house,

who dug deep and laid the foundation on the rock. And when a flood arose, the stream broke against that house and could not shake it, because it had been well built. But the one who hears and does not do them is like a man who built a house on the ground without a foundation. When the stream broke against it, immediately it fell, and the ruin of that house was great.

This devotional is a thirty-day journey of revelations in the areas of inner healing, deliverance, mind renewal, prayer, fear of the Lord, and worship, all of which were discovered in my secret place.

Although I write about these topics separately, I find they are all interconnected, because a spirit-led life is never compartmentalized. It is like a river, the flow of which is directed by the Lord's guidance and presence.

My prayer is that this devotional will provide meaningful insights, encouragement, and guidance to help you lay a solid foundation to equip you for your future. I pray it offers inspiration, wisdom, and practical advice to empower you as you prepare for what lies ahead.

Section 1

Inner Healing

You will never see yourself until you see Jesus. We are the reflection of the wounds that He bore for us. He was wounded so we could be healed.

"But He was wounded for our transgressions, He was bruised for our guilt and iniquities; the chastisement [needful to obtain] peace and well-being for us was upon Him, and with the stripes [that wounded] Him we are healed and made whole."

Isaiah 53:5, AMPC

There are moments in our spiritual journey when God will lead us through a season that defines us. For me, that season was in 2023 when I lost my dad to suicide. It was the most intense pain, loss, and grief I have ever experienced.

It shook me to the core. It challenged my identity, authority, and assignment. However, my proximity to the presence of God and guidance from the Holy Spirit helped me to attain a deeper level of intimacy and dependency on God. This revoked the enemy's attempt to undermine the character and nature of God. Moreover, it revealed my position as God's daughter, seated with Him in the heavenly places.

Before this defining season, my family and I had faced multiple seasons of distress, trauma, and transition. During these difficult times, I did not properly grieve and process the pain, which left me with a lingering sense of grief and trauma. However, during this defining season, God worked through my experiences to help me fully release the pain, grief, and trauma that I had carried with me for so long.

Despite being spiritually liberated and free in my mind, my body still bore the physical scars of pain and trauma. Several medical conditions had taken root in my body, impeding my quality of life and causing discomfort.

One night, I drove a long distance to attend a meeting. I said, "Lord, I want to be healed of this trauma manifesting in my body. I believe it will go tonight."

At that meeting, as everyone worshiped in one accord and ministered to the Lord, I suddenly had a vision of grabbing Jesus's face. I said, "Jesus, I want to see you."

As I gazed into His eyes, I remembered the compassion and love I saw. Even His lower lids brimmed with tears as He looked at me. Then, suddenly, He stretched out His hands, became vulnerable, and invited me in close, saying, "Dana, I want you to touch my wounds with your wounds."

I saw His nail-pierced hands and couldn't resist touching them with my own. And then, something incredible happened: the wounds in His hands turned into mirrors. When I looked into them, I saw my own reflection and realized that I was completely whole. It was an experience I will never forget.

Jesus said, "Dana, you have been made whole. Now, live from that place."

I was overwhelmed by the encounter. I can testify the pain left my body, and my physical ailments ceased. I have health reports to prove it.

If you can see Him, you will see yourself. We are the reflection of the wounds that He suffered. It can be painful, but on the other side of His wounds lies complete healing. Jesus has already made the provision for our spiritual, mental, emotional, and physical healing. We can now take every area that is broken and surrender it to the cross.

I pray for a transformative encounter with Jesus and the profound work that was accomplished on the cross as we begin to navigate the journey of inner healing.

Day 1

The Enemy's Greatest Tactic is to Unseat the Soul.

I believe that one of the most crucial questions we should ask ourselves regularly is, "How is my soul?" I am very intentional about taking extra time to focus on my soul health. Through this, God has shown me that the enemy's primary tactic is to distract, sidetrack, steal, kill, and destroy our joy. His main goal is to unseat our soul, which is our place of power and prosperity. This is because he knows we prosper as our soul prospers.

Every day, I go to my secret place, close the door, and patiently wait for the Lord's leading. Often, I sit at the table with Jesus and receive His body and blood through communion. I lift my hands in praise and thanksgiving because giving God the highest honor is an act of warfare that confuses and frustrates the enemy's plans.

I pray by grabbing my journal, listening, and allowing God's voice to speak into any area where I am not finding rest or peace. I let Him reveal inner conflict, worry, or anxious thoughts. I repent and release them to the cross. As I let go of these burdens, I receive His peace.

Finally, I choose to stay in that peaceful place and meditate on this promise found in John 14:27 (TPT):

> I leave the gift of peace with you—my peace. Not the kind of fragile peace given by the world, but my perfect peace. Don't yield to fear or be troubled in your hearts—instead, be courageous!

Did you know God gave you emotions, feelings, and thoughts because they can alert you to areas of pain and trauma that need His healing power? Your emotions and pain are essential to Him because He is the God of wholeness. Therefore, bring your pain with you and draw closer to Him, as He wants to transform it into joy.

John 10:9–10 (TPT) says:

> I am the Gateway. To enter through me is to experience life, freedom, and satisfaction. A thief has only one thing in mind—he wants to steal, slaughter, and destroy. But I have come to give you everything in abundance, more than you expect—life in its fullness until you overflow!

How is your soul? Take a moment to evaluate it today because the state of your soul is extremely valuable to our Father.

Prayer

Holy Spirit, I invite you into the hidden, painful places of my heart. I ask that you come in and tenderize the places where I am calloused. Shine your light and expose the darkness. I give you my pain by choosing not to hold on to it. Instead, I allow you, Holy Spirit, my comforter, to reconcile the pain, and I lay it at the foot of the cross. I receive your healing, your peace, and your joy. In Jesus' name, Amen.

Key Scriptures

John 14:27 (TPT); John 10:9–10 (TPT)

Day 2

Is Staying The Same More Painful Than The Journey And Commitment It Will Take to Get Well?

Wounds untreated will cost more in the long run than the journey to healing them.

In John 5:1–9 (TPT), it is recorded that Jesus encountered a man with a disability at the Pool of Bethesda. This particular pool was believed to have healing powers, as the angel of God would stir the waters, and whoever entered the pool during this moment would receive healing. As a result, hundreds of sick people were healed in these waters daily.

For thirty-eight years, there was a man who lived with a victim mentality. He was born with a disability, and every day, he waited for someone to take responsibility for him, help him get into the pool and lower him down so that he could be healed.

Jesus arrived at the scene, already aware of the man's prolonged condition. Despite his limitations, He asked the man, "Do you truly long to be well?"

The man's initial response was to replay the last thirty-eight years of an infirmity-filled life, the life of a victim, and place the blame on everyone else who didn't help him get into the pool.

Ignoring his symptoms, Jesus said to him, "Stand up! Pick up your sleeping mat, and you will walk!"

Perhaps Jesus understood that a man's true desire for healing is greater than the pain of remaining a victim. Jesus' only requirement was faith. In one moment of faith, this man's choice to get up out of his victim state and walk as a victor changed the entire trajectory of his life. A thirty-eight-year struggle ended when the man had a revelation that he did not need to stay in that condition anymore.

Where is Jesus asking you to pick up your mat? Will you choose to stay a victim or stand up as a victor? We are *made* well only by Jesus, not the control of our circumstances.

Perhaps you are not physically disabled but emotionally disabled because of unresolved pain, trauma, grief, discouragement, or disappointment.

Avoiding emotional pain may provide temporary relief, but it can lead to a lifetime of suffering. It will cause you to live life from a wound instead of from victory.

When we fail to confront our emotions, we limit our capacity for growth and healing. As a result, we may find ourselves building walls around our hearts instead of reaching out to build healthy relationships. This can cause us to keep our distance from those we love and even from God.

God desires you to have meaningful, intimate relationships with Him, yourself, and others.

Picking up your mat, confronting your pain, and moving toward healing is difficult, but it is necessary to live a victorious life. These things take time, so take the time.

Allow God to bring these things up His way, which is always healthy. Take your Father's hand and ask *Him* to help you take an internal look that goes far beneath the surface. Let *Him* come in and restore health and intimacy once again.

This is the best thing I have ever done for myself and for the loved ones around me. What He has done for me, He will do for you.

Prayer

Jesus, I surrender my affliction and my pain to you. I repent for trying to control my circumstances, pain, and for living as a victim when you shed your precious blood to make me a victor. I renounce every agreement with doubt and unbelief. I take this step of faith to move toward my healing. I shift off the weights that have hindered my healing, pick up my mat, and move toward the finished work of the cross. Thank you for healing my body, soul, and spirit so that I can live from victory to victory. In Jesus' name, Amen.

Key Scriptures

John 5:1–9 (TPT)

Day 3

When Pain or Grief Comes, Remember Not to Focus on The Pain or Grief, But The One Who Bore Your Pain And Grief.

The Holy Spirit whispered the statement of the title above one morning as I sat with Him to prepare for the day.

During difficult times, it can be easy to go down the rabbit hole of sorrow or self-pity. However, Jesus was known as the Man of Sorrows so we do not have to be.

Although pain and suffering are real, we should not allow them to consume our lives and define our identity. Instead, we can find solace in Jesus amid the struggles.

One of the most painful experiences I have ever had was losing my father unexpectedly to suicide in 2023. The grief was overwhelming and unlike anything I had ever experienced before.

I had to be aggressive and very intentional about surrendering that trauma and pain to God.

If I had allowed the pain and grief to consume my life and not surrendered them to God, they would have turned into self-pity, fear, depression, hopelessness, mistrust, and unbelief. Before I knew it, I would have been completely isolated, disillusioned, and disconnected from God and people.

I had to guard my heart and not let unyielded pain and grief become a substitute for God.

I didn't try to fix that area of my life on my own, but instead, I opened myself up to God's presence and guidance through seeking intimacy with Him and connecting with a community of faith.

Psalms 84:5–7 (MSG) sums it up beautifully:

> And how blessed all those in whom you live, whose lives become roads you travel; They wind through lonesome valleys, come upon brooks, discover cool springs and pools brimming with rain! God-traveled, these roads curve up the mountain, and at the last turn—Zion! God in full view!

I love how Paul puts it to the Macedonians in 2 Corinthians 7:11–13 (MSG):

> And now, isn't it wonderful all the ways in which this distress has goaded you closer to God? You're more alive, more concerned, more sensitive, more reverent, more human, more passionate, more responsible. Looked at from any angle, you've come out of this with purity of heart. And that is what I was hoping for in the first place when I wrote the letter.

When we face worldly distress, hurt, disappointments, or pain, if we manage them correctly, they can help us cultivate purity of heart.

When we face the challenges of life, we can find hope in the truth that Jesus took the ultimate blow for us, allowing us to surrender everything at the foot of the cross.

When I give Jesus what I am unable to carry, I can feel the supernatural strength that only His resurrection power can give.

In Psalm 51:7–12 (ESV), David writes, "Purge me with hyssop, and I shall be clean; wash me, and I shall be whiter than snow." Hyssop was a cleansing agent that symbolized deliverance, healing, and comfort.

He continues in verses 8–12:

> Let me hear joy and gladness; let the bones that you have broken rejoice. Hide your face from my sins, and blot out all my iniquities. Create in me a clean heart, O God, and renew a right spirit within me. Cast me not away from your presence, and take not your Holy Spirit from me. Restore to me the joy of your salvation, and uphold me with a willing spirit.

What areas of your life have you been carrying heavy burdens of pain and grief that you need to surrender to Jesus?

Prayer

Dear Jesus, I come to you with the pain and grief that I have been holding on to. I recognize my need for your help and that I cannot do this on my own. I know that hiding my pain and grief will not heal it, and I do not want this to control my life anymore. I repent for not trusting you and trying to control pain instead of confronting it. I see you on the cross and that you took all my pain, sickness, and grief upon yourself, purchasing my victory. I now release this to you. Holy Spirit, I ask that you come in and comfort me in this place. Help me to choose the love and comfort of Jesus instead of the comfort of pain and grief. Anoint me with the oil of joy and gladness. In Jesus' name, Amen.

Key Scriptures

Psalms 84:5–7 (MSG); 2 Corinthians 7:11–13 (MSG); Psalm 51:7–12 (ESV)

Day 4

Pain is a Journey, Not a Destination. Don't Build an Idol Where You Were Meant to Build an Altar.

I want to remind someone today that pain is a part of the journey. You will only grow to the level of your pain threshold. *But* it is not a destination.

If we do not learn how to navigate seasons of pain or unforeseen circumstances properly, we will build idols where we were meant to build altars. We will become calloused where we were meant to become tender.

We will become sick in our souls when we worship our pain, grief, and sackcloth more than we worship God. We will become victims instead of overcoming as victors.

A victim wakes up every day and rehearses defeat. A victim becomes powerless and thinks that they cannot do anything about the things that have happened to them.

Victims often attribute blame to others instead of taking responsibility for their actions. Instead of living a fruitful life, victims live frustrated. Victims always demand something. A victim cannot reciprocate; a victim always takes.

Living as a victim will lead you into a lifestyle of self-preservation and isolation.

A person who has unhealed wounds will become easily offended or triggered anytime someone, like a Godly friend or pastor, or something, like a circumstance, pushes on wounds that remind them of their past experiences.

When someone has a physical wound, their first instinct is to cover the wound to protect it and prevent others from touching it to avoid the risk of being hurt again. Physical wounds are easy to see and identify.

The wounds of the soul can work in the same way as physical wounds, but they are internal. Initially, they are subtle, until they start to govern a person's life.

The person with a soul wound will try to manage their pain through their emotions to suppress it. As a result, they tend to be emotionally reactive, which affects their thoughts and behaviors.

If the person does not resolve the pain God's way, walls will be erected in their heart.

The person who fails to deal with their wounds will eventually become isolated. Their wounds will continue to fester, preventing them from forming deep, meaningful relationships.

Unfortunately, the undealt-with wounds not only afflict that person, but the people around them. The festering wounds begin to infect every area of their life. Hurt people will hurt people, and these people will begin to bleed on others.

But the truth is God wants to heal the broken heart and emotions because God loves relationships. His heart is that people enjoy the right relationships.

He wants people to pass through the valley and journey through the pain so that they can become a wellspring that blesses others.

David paints a beautiful picture of this in Psalms 84:6–7 (TPT):

> Even when their paths wind through the dark valley of tears, they dig deep to find a pleasant pool *where others find only pain*. He gives to them a brook of blessing filled from the rain of an outpouring. They grow stronger and stronger with every step forward, and the God of all gods will appear before them in Zion.

Perhaps you sense that there is something blocking the flow of intimacy between you, God, and others. Ask the Holy Spirit to highlight any areas where there may be walls, undealt-with wounds, or areas that you are operating in self-preservation.

Prayer

Holy Spirit, I invite you to come in, search my heart and examine it. Let the light of God shine into the dark places where there is repressed pain. Show me where I have not taken responsibility for the pain, hurting both myself and others. Show me where I have become spiritually dull, blind, and deaf because of wounds that are blocking intimacy and my ability to rightly see and hear. I ask you, Lord, the great physician and surgeon, to take your scalpel and cut away these places. Forgive me for holding on to these areas instead of surrendering them to you. I renounce and break every soul tie of control, and I come into complete covenant with you. I allow you, Holy Spirit, to help me, and allow the ones that you send to speak into my life. I commit to the journey of healing and give up my rights to stay stuck in my wounds. Thank you for your guidance and for helping me. In Jesus' name, Amen.

Key Scriptures

Psalms 84:6–7 (TPT)

Day 5

The Ultimate Fruit of Healing is Self-Control.

The antithesis of fear and control are power, love, and self-control.

2 Timothy 1:7 (AMP) says:

> For God did not give us a spirit of timidity or cowardice or fear, but [He has given us a spirit] of power and of love and of sound judgment and personal discipline [abilities that result in a calm, well-balanced mind and self-control].

Proverbs 29:11 (ESV) says, "A fool gives full vent to his spirit, but a wise man quietly holds it back."

The opposite of exercising your opinion is to restrain it through self-control. Some of the wisest people I have encountered are skilled listeners who speak less and only provide their opinion when requested. When you can do this, it is the fruit of self-control and inner healing.

Paul boldly makes it plain in 1 Corinthians 10:23 (NIV):

> "I have the right to do anything," you say—but not everything is beneficial. "I have the right to do anything"—but not everything is constructive.

When we react to a situation, we let our emotions take control. Consequently, we are more likely to become defensive and say hurtful things.

Many people react because of unprocessed emotions that are not healed. Emotional bondage causes people to focus on what is wrong with them and project it onto others.

If you focus on yourself, it becomes all about you. You criticize yourself and become critical of others.

You live your life from a wound, and instead of empowering people, you bleed on them.

Responding, however, involves developing a thoughtful response that is guided by God's truth more than our emotions. Responding results from shifting our focus on what is right with God, and He becomes our focus.

Ultimately, when you are healed, you will use the fruit of self-control to respond to situations, not react.

The more intimate we become with God, the less we want to live with our wrongs. We naturally surrender to Him, knowing He is bigger than our struggles.

True healing and self-control will be displayed in your life because the conversation in your head and the words that come out of your mouth will sound better, and not bitter.

Do you get the last word, or does God?

Do not let the enemy use you against yourself because it does not just impact you; it impacts those around you.

If he can take your joy, he takes your power and prosperity. Let us decide to focus on how right God is and watch as you prosper in all things and be in good health as your soul prospers.

Where are the areas in your life where you have unsettled, repressed emotions, causing you to react instead of respond? Let us bring those to the cross today.

Prayer

Lord, I come before you today and completely surrender this emotion that I am experiencing. Holy Spirit, I invite you in to help me recognize how I am feeling. I know my emotions are an indicator, but they are not the truth. Holy Spirit, I ask that you come in and help me reconcile this emotion and how it makes me feel. Give me the strength to completely submit it to Jesus so that I am empowered to overcome. This emotion does not rule over me. This emotion does not control me, sabotaging my relationship with you, myself, and others. I give you this emotion and thank you for reigning over this and every area of my life allowing me to grow in power, love, and self-control. In Jesus' name, Amen.

Key Scriptures

2 Timothy 1:7 (AMP); Proverbs 29:11 (ESV); 1 Corinthians 10:23 (NIV)

Section 2

Deliverance

Every family has a deliverer who repairs the breach and rebuilds the walls of ruin; it might as well be you.

"And your ancient ruins shall be rebuilt; you shall raise up the foundations of many generations; you shall be called the repairer of the breach, the restorer of streets to dwell in."

Isaiah 58:12, ESV

There is a type of reconciliation and restoration that can only come from God. There is a level of obedience and integrity to do the right thing that can only come from the strength God gives.

In Genesis 44 and 45 (NIV), we witness Joseph's greatest act of reconciliation with his family. Not only does he forgive his brothers, but he also provides for them.

In Genesis 45:7 (NIV), his words were, "But God sent me ahead of you to preserve for you a remnant on earth and to save your lives by a great deliverance."

When Pharoah heard this, he provided for them also. In Genesis 45:27 (NIV), when they told Joseph's father, Jacob, the Bible says, "his spirit was revived."

It is important to remember that people are watching how you manage injustice. Your response does not just affect you; it has an impact on everyone around you.

Proverbs 13:12 (NIV) says, "Hope deferred makes the heart sick, but a longing fulfilled is a tree of life."

Like Joseph, I prayed for reconciliation in my family, especially my relationship with my mom, for twenty years. Then suddenly, in a moment, God took what seemed dead and restored it back to life and vitality. It feels like that dark season never existed because of how God completely removed it.

I hope my story and the story of Joseph inspire you to be the one that goes first in your family. Rely on God's strength, and do what is right, and He will fulfill His promises.

As we move on to the next section, my prayer is that you will not only be liberated from the influence of evil and the contamination of sin, but also that your life will radiate the same resurrection power that raised Christ Jesus from the dead, overflowing into the lives of those around you.

Day 1

Your Freedom And Your Transformation Are 100% Your Responsibility.

If everyone had this simple revelation, we would turn the world upside down.

It is one thing to be set free, but it is entirely another thing to live free.

Many people are delivered and set free in a moment of power, but if they do not know how to stay free, they may continue to make the same choices. Sometimes, people's situations do not improve, and instead worsen because of the consequences of their choices.

Matthew 12:28–30 (MSG) says:

> But if it's by God's power that I am sending the evil spirits packing, then God's kingdom is here for sure. How in the world do you think it's possible in broad daylight to enter the house of an awake, able-bodied man and walk off with his possessions unless you tie him up first? Tie him up, though, and you can clean him out. This is war, and there is no neutral ground. If you're not on my side, you're the enemy; if you're not helping, you're making things worse.

You can be your own worst enemy!

If you sow things of the flesh, you will reap things of the flesh. However, if you sow things of the spirit, you will reap things of the spirit.

I need to be truthful and say that freedom is not a destination; it is a journey. Freedom is a process and lifetime commitment to living free.

The altar is not a one-stop shop where you leave the altar and your part is done. It is quite the opposite. When you leave the altar, your part has just begun. The rest of your freedom journey is about staying on that altar in your personal life.

Your freedom and your transformation are 100% your responsibility. Your leaders are not responsible for your transformation; they are responsible for your discipleship.

Freedom can be confrontational, so it takes faith to walk it out. Freedom is a journey of progress, not perfection.

Romans 4:7-8 (TPT) says:

> What happy fulfillment is ahead for those whose rebellion has been forgiven and whose sins are covered by blood. What happy progress comes to them when they hear the Lord speak over them, "I will never hold your sins against you!"

What if everyone committed to taking responsibility for their own journey to freedom, and took the next steps no matter where they are in the process?

Take some time to sit with the Holy Spirit and ask what your next steps are in your freedom journey.

Some questions you can ask are:

Holy Spirit, where are the areas I have not taken responsibility for in my freedom journey?

Holy Spirit, have I unknowingly opened any doorways, allowing the thief to gain legal access, oppress me, and steal my freedom?

Holy Spirit, where are the areas in my heart where I have built idols instead of intimacy? Have I allowed idols of fear, control, rejection, bitterness, unforgiveness, or addiction to comfort me instead of you?

Holy Spirit, are there strongholds in my mind where I have built belief systems of limitation?

Prayer

Holy Spirit, I surrender my heart and invite you to come in. Search me and expose the areas that are broken, oppressed, or where I have made agreements with lies. I repent (be specific about the area of sin or agreement) and bring it to the cross. I renounce all agreements that I have made with (be specific about the stronghold) and where I have given the enemy a foothold to oppress me. I break these covenants and replace them with the blood of Jesus. In Jesus' name, I take authority and command every unclean spirit to be uprooted. I command every demonic curse sent against my life to be broken in Jesus' name! I declare every curse sent against my life to be reversed by the blood of Jesus. I receive every work of the cross and all the benefits. In Jesus' name, Amen.

Key Scriptures

Matthew 12:28–30 (MSG); Romans 4:7–8 (TPT)

Day 2

If You Consume More Than You Produce, You Will Always Live in a Deficit; Beggars Always Borrow.

God has led me on a journey of studying the spirit of poverty, one of the most destructive forces of all time.

Jesus warned His disciples in Matthew 26:11 (NKJV) about this, saying, "For you have the poor with you always, but Me you do not have always."

Jesus was not talking about money, but the condition of the soul.

Poverty comes from living life as a victim. The reality is lack of money is a late sign. Before poverty influences a person's wallet, it has already been influencing a person's life.

Lack is the language and the fruit of a victim. You can recognize a poverty spirit when the person fails to take responsibility and expects others to do so.

The prevailing spirit of our time is one of poverty. This spirit seeks to weaken people, so they lack the strength and ability to bear the weight of responsibility. When a person cannot carry this weight, they are unable to wield spiritual weapons. Without the use of spiritual weapons, they are unable to influence others. When a person lacks influence, they end up with the least amount of power and authority.

As Christians, we need to disciple others and help them access the power that can destroy the spirit of lack, and enable them to live in abundance, bless others, and disciple them in return.

In the gospels, there are several instances where people were affected by poverty that resulted in disability. Three such examples can be found in the stories of the man at the pool of Bethesda in John 5:1–15 (NKJV), the man at the gate called Beautiful in Acts 3:1–10 (NKJV), and the story of Blind Bartimaeus in Mark 10:46–52 (TPT).

All of these men were impoverished beggars who had turned their temporary condition into a lifestyle.

The story of the man who was crippled for thirty-eight years at the Pool of Bethesda teaches us that he was only healed when he stopped waiting on someone else for healing and instead, responded in obedience to Jesus. By picking up his mat and walking, he was healed in an instant.

The man who sat at the Beautiful Gate was dragged there every day to beg for charitable donations. One day, he met Peter and John, who said, "Silver and gold I do not have, but what I do have I give you: In the name of Jesus Christ of Nazareth, rise up and walk."

The man put his hands in theirs, took responsibility, and had faith. In that moment, he was given the ability to do what he had never done before—he could walk!

Blind Bartimaeus, whose name meant "highly prized," was a blind beggar until he met Jesus in Jericho. All he had to do was ignore the crowd and hear Jesus. Above the crowd, he shouted, "Jesus, son of David, have mercy on me now in my affliction. Heal me!"

The Bible says he threw off his beggar's cloak, jumped up, and made his way to Jesus. He asked Jesus to let him see. This act was a declaration of the man's faith that he was not defined by his affliction and that he could see himself healed.

Jesus responded, "Your faith heals you. Go in peace, with your sight restored."

All at once, his eyes were opened. He received it because he first believed.

Jesus and His disciples did not minister through handouts, which would leave people worse. Instead, they empowered them to move to the next level of faith.

Every miracle performed during Jesus' ministry required the participation of the people in faith. When they acted in faith, they received the power of resurrection that would heal them.

He turned beggars into believers by asking them to participate in their own miracle. We need to cancel the culture of borrowing and put on our faith pants.

What areas are you living impoverished, areas that require resurrection power to help you stand up today?

Prayer

Lord, I open my heart to you today realizing that the issues of my life are directly correlated to the condition of my heart. Lord, I recognize that I have been adopted into a royal kingdom as (a son or a daughter), but I have been living like an orphan. I bring this to the cross and repent for mindsets of poverty, lack, complacency, apathy, isolation, and trying to do things on my own. I repent for living like a victim when you paid the highest price for me to live from victory. I renounce all agreements with lack and poverty. I receive every spiritual blessing in the heavenly realm and the inheritance that you purchased for me. I pick up my mat,

I take your hand, and in faith, I move toward the miracles that you have preordained for me. In Jesus' name, Amen.

Key Scriptures

Matthew 26:11 (NKJV); John 5:1–15 (NKJV); Acts 3:1–10 (NKJV); Mark 10:46–52 (TPT)

Day 3

True Healing Doesn't Happen Until We Surrender Our Disease.

One of Jesus' most impactful questions was, "Do you want to be made well?"

His "next step" was always "go and sin no more." In other words, "break your agreements with the lies that you have been living."

Living under a curse can lead to sickness.

When you choose to break curses, agreements, and lies, you can reprogram your mind back to its default setting: the perception of Christ.

The outcome of living your life on God's terms is a blessed and fruitful life.

Throughout my early adult life, I lived with an orphan mindset. Because of the chaos I experienced in my home as a child, I believed I had to make it on my own and provide for myself. I built walls to control the pain of not feeling protected and provided for, which blocked the flow of God's blessing.

I kept the pain close through self-preservation and self-dependence, which led me to keep God and people at a distance. This kept me isolated.

Although I had received freedom in this area and believed I had moved past this issue, my father's tragic death revealed roots that were still present.

Besides God and my husband, Joel, there was no man I loved more than my father. When I lost him, the chaos of this tragedy spun everything out of control.

As a result, instead of trusting God, I started to operate in lack. My mind was consumed not only by the grief of losing my father, but also by the fear of an uncertain future and the possibility of not having, or ever having, enough.

Because of the fear, I began to operate in control and decided I was the one who had to provide for our household. I began to overstep my husband and God.

One day, I found myself emotionally exhausted and came to the end of myself. While I was journaling the "fruit" of what I was seeing in my life in my secret place, the Holy Spirit showed me the "root."

All the symptoms indicated I was operating in an orphan mindset. The Holy Spirit revealed to me that as a child, even though my physical needs were provided for, I was not provided for emotionally. As a result, I began to work because I needed to have some sense of control over my life.

I started working early to provide for myself. Unfortunately, this caused me to miss many opportunities to play sports and enjoy life. I was constantly striving to perform and provide for myself, using it as a coping mechanism.

After the Holy Spirit revealed it to me, I realized I was reverting to childhood patterns to maintain control during chaos. I used this as a coping mechanism so I did not have to feel out of control.

Immediately, I renounced the spirit of fear, renounced all agreements made with poverty, lack, and the orphan mindset. I broke the soul ties attached to control and came into covenant with Jesus. As a result, God took His position as my provider and protector, which allowed my husband to do the same.

The moment I surrendered my "dis"ease and released control, everything changed.

My eyes were opened, and I experienced the true revelation that God does not create pain or "dis"ease. Instead, He uses it to help us heal every issue of the heart and any limitation that keeps us from walking in the inheritance that He has already provided through Jesus.

In John 14:27 (NKJV), Jesus says, "Peace I leave with you, My peace I give to you; not as the world gives do I give to you. Let not your heart be troubled, neither let it be afraid."

Again, in John 16:33 (NKJV), He reinforces the message of peace by saying, "These things I have spoken to you, that in Me you may have peace. In the world you will have tribulation; but be of good cheer, I have overcome the world."

These scriptures are saying that living in a fallen world can bring pressures, conflicts, and turmoil. Jesus experienced these same difficulties, but He had the power to overcome.

God promises that through Jesus, we have the power to break perpetual cycles of defeat and become victorious.

What areas of your life have you come into agreement with "dis"ease and have been reluctant to accept the offer of God's true healing? What areas of your life do you experience worry, anxiety, and fear instead of the perfect peace that Jesus offers? Surrender it to God today. He is the same yesterday, today, and forever.

Prayer

Jesus, I come to you in complete surrender. I surrender my mind, will, and emotions to you. I surrender my control. I ask, Holy Spirit, that you search my heart and reveal the areas that I have built walls where you want to bring love and intimacy. I ask that your perfect peace and your unconditional love flood into those areas and remove the blockages. I receive your healing, your blessing, and I step into the life that you have for me. Help me to live from that place so that I may bring refreshment and life to others. In Jesus' name, Amen.

Key Scriptures

John 14:27 (NKJV); John 16:33 (NKJV)

Day 4

What Sin is Seducing You?

This may not be the sexiest topic, but it is an important one that requires discussion.

Is it that juicy gossip you just cannot resist at the office? Is it the second or third drink that leaves you feeling heavy the next day? Is it the people you slander instead of honor?

Proverbs contains key scriptures that address not only sexual sin, but any sin that leads to bondage.

Proverbs 5:8–9 (TPT) says:

Don't even go near the door of her house unless you want to fall into her seduction. In disgrace you will relinquish your honor to another, and all your remaining years will be squandered—given over to the cruel one.

Later in Proverbs 7:25-27 (TPT), we are asked a sobering question:

> Why would you want to even get close to temptation and seduction, to have an affair with her? She has pierced the souls of multitudes of men—many mighty ones have fallen and have been brought down by her. If you're looking for the road to hell, just go looking for her house!

Both the kingdom of God and the kingdom of darkness operate under a legal system. When we continually engage in sinful behavior and violate God's laws, it creates openings that allow demons to gain legal permission to enter and stay in our lives.

Doors have locks for a reason. Robbers are attracted to houses where doors are unlocked.

Doorways stay open or reopen through unforgiveness, anger, fear, control, bitterness, complaining, gossiping, rebellion, sexual sin, living an alternative lifestyle, addiction, and worshiping idols that substitute God—just to name a few.

Because of the lack of belief in the authority of the Word of God, many continue to fall into the seduction of sin because they put their faith in sin and not the Word of God.

When you understand the authority of the Word of God and its power over sin, the Word of God will lead you instead of rescuing you.

A double-edged sword is meant to pierce you and your opponent.

In Matthew 4 (NKJV), the Bible says that after fasting forty days and nights, Jesus was led into the wilderness to face the devil, who tried to seduce Him three times. Each time, Jesus responded with, "It is written."

He also stated, "Man does not live by bread alone, but by every word that proceeds from the mouth of God."

Jesus illustrated the ability to overcome the temptation to feed His flesh even when He was hungry. He demonstrated complete submission and obedience to His Father by waiting on the timing of His ministry. He did not "jump ahead" in disobedience, then ask His Father to protect

Him. Finally, He proved Himself a true worshiper by not bowing His knee to the shiny things or substitutions for God.

The Word spoke the Word. With that authority, He resisted the devil, causing the devil to flee. Angels were then dispatched to minister to Him.

James 4:7–10 (MSG) is a great template to overcoming the temptation to sin:

> So let God work his will in you. Yell a loud no to the Devil and watch him make himself scarce. Say a quiet yes to God and he'll be there in no time. Quit dabbling in sin. Purify your inner life. Quit playing the field. Hit bottom, and cry your eyes out. The fun and games are over. Get serious, really serious. Get down on your knees before the Master; it's the only way you'll get on your feet.

What areas are you stuck? What areas has the Holy Spirit been nudging you to stop crouching near the door of sin's seduction? Take action today to break agreements with the lie. Do not give any legal ground for demons to access your life.

Prayer

Lord, I repent of the perpetual cycle of sin I have been in and renounce every agreement I have made with its lies. I elevate the name of Jesus to the highest place of authority over every power of darkness. By the power of the Holy Spirit, I take authority and command every unclean spirit to be uprooted.

In Jesus' name, I bind and break every spirit of fear, anxiety, depression, rejection, condemnation, and religion. I renounce every soul tie covenant made through manipulation, witchcraft, control, sexual sin, and perversion. I break these covenants and replace them with the blood of Jesus. In Jesus' name, Amen.

Key Scriptures

Proverbs 5:8–9 (TPT); Proverbs 7:25–27 (TPT); Matthew 4 (NKJV); James 4:7–10 (MSG)

Day 5

Warfare is The Key to Possession and Required For Ownership to Change.

It is time to stop giving the devil a paycheck on Jesus' dime. It is time for the people of God to possess their possessions.

We see patents of God's plan for us to take possession all throughout the Old Testament.

In Deuteronomy 1 (ESV), the Israelites were on an eleven-day journey that took them forty years because they stayed stuck in a wilderness, frustrated, when they were meant to go in and take possession.

So, God delivers His word to Moses, saying, "You have stayed long enough at this mountain. Turn and take your journey."

Further down in Deuteronomy 1:8, he says, "See, I have set the land before you. Go in and take possession of the land that the Lord swore to your fathers, to Abraham, to Isaac, and to Jacob."

Later in the Book of Joshua, we see the sequel to the possession of the land. The sequel is that the Israelites continued to encounter resistance even after they had settled in the land.

The heart of God was to empower them to never just settle. Their responsibility was to displace every stronghold and take possession of each territory that remained.

There will always be more territory in your heart that needs to be conquered, even if God has set you free or healed you in one area.

Moreover, there is territory in other people's hearts that He needs you to help them possess. You have authority in the area that you have overcome.

The enemy's number-one tactic is to destroy you or disqualify you in the very place that you were meant to possess.

In my personal journey, it was the area of family. God called me to save the lives of preborn children and end the trauma of abortion, but I came from a lineage of generational dysfunction and mental illness. I was almost aborted through medical negligence, and I lost my dad to suicide in 2023.

I've had encounters where the devil tried to condemn me, saying, "Who are you to rebuild the family unit? You couldn't even save your own!"

But no sooner were those words spoken when I heard the voice of God say, "You are proof that the curse has been broken. Now, stand in your identity, and go possess the land!"

I had the honor of working for a pro-life clinic for five years that once shared a wall with the second largest abortion clinic in San Diego. When the abortion clinic shut down, we took possession of it in 2022. This action set a precedent to continue shutting down all abortion clinics and taking possession of them until they are all occupied by the kingdom of God.

I never would have been able to be a part of taking this territory if I could not see past my history. If I remained fixated on my past, I would have bowed my knee to the idols of fear and intimidation, which were never going to give me permission to go in and possess.

If the thief comes, he can no longer steal. In fact, he will labor because I give no opportunity to the devil. I stand in my office, in the assignment God has given me and my identity as His daughter.

Romans 8:15 (AMP) says:

> For you have not received a spirit of slavery leading again to fear [of God's judgment], but you have received the Spirit of adoption as sons [the Spirit producing sonship].

If you search for the word "son," you will find that it comes from the word "ben," which means "to build." Sons (ben) or daughters (bena) build their Father's house. They represent and reveal to men the nature, heart, and character of God. They are a generational extension of the Father, and they cause His kingdom to continue.

As a daughter, I must take responsibility for every stronghold because it is difficult to experience the fullness of the benefits of being a builder if you function in a kingdom that opposes it.

When we allow God to free us from strongholds in exchange for the spirit of sonship, we no longer operate from slavery and religious duty, but from our God-given identity. We become generous and life-giving like our Father.

We build His house and our lives the way He wants us to build them.

When our lives become an expression of our identity as sons and daughters, it is amazing how much we enjoy our freedom and serving others. It is amazing to see the risks we will take.

God will continue to give us big assignments that He is faithful to resource. When you are a builder, you will never be a beggar.

Personally, I have witnessed the flow of blessing over my life. I have learned that when you build with God, you get to inherit what you build. I have inherited homes, a kingdom marriage, radical restoration of family, and miracles in deliverance, as well as witnessed numerous testimonies of the healing of the sick.

We are sons and daughters. The world desperately needs us to awaken to our identity, break strongholds, and build God's kingdom on Earth.

What areas of your life are you stuck in that you know you need to move forward in obedience, to go in and take possession? What are the areas that you know you lack the revelation of who you are in Christ? Let us stand in our identity and take possession of these areas today.

Prayer

Lord, I come to you, and I am aware that I have been stuck. I repent for allowing the enemy to trespass on the land that you have given me to possess in my heart and my God-given assignment. I renounce every agreement I have made with fear, intimidation, and complacency. I repent for living under the curse of slavery instead of the freedom of being a (son or daughter). I rise, stand in my office, and my God-given assignment. I take authority over every principality and ruler and command every tormentor to loosen your hold on my life. I belong to Jesus. I put off the old man and put on the new self. I do not walk in the futility of my mind, alienated from a full life with you. I put on the new man created after your likeness in true righteousness and holiness. I ask for a fresh impartation of courage to continue to possess, occupy, and disrupt the kingdom of darkness. In Jesus' name, Amen.

Key Scriptures

Deuteronomy 1:1–8 (ESV); Romans 8:15 (AMP)

Section 3

Mind Renewal

You are as set free and as healed as your mind is renewed.

"Be *continually* renewed in the spirit of your mind [having a fresh, untarnished mental and spiritual attitude], and put on the new self [the regenerated and renewed nature], created in God's image, [godlike] in the righteousness and holiness of the truth [living in a way that expresses to God your gratitude for your salvation]."

Ephesians 4:23–24, AMP

You may not be able to control the thoughts you think, but you can choose the thoughts you accept.

One of the most powerful tools that we can have in our spiritual arsenal to maintain freedom is the weapon of mind renewal.

There is a war constantly being waged in the mind. The outcome of each battle depends on the weapons used.

We cannot fight grown-up battles with teenage tactics. If we use the same weapons as unbelievers, we will achieve the same outcomes.

2 Corinthians 10:4 (NKJV) says, "For the weapons of our warfare are not carnal but mighty in God for pulling down strongholds."

The Word of God has the power to bring down strongholds, renew the mind, and rebuild old belief systems.

Wounds of the soul, especially if they came about through a person's formative years, can become deeply embedded or leave an impression in their inner man (their mind, will, and emotions.) The deeper the embedding, the longer it may take to heal and reprogram the belief system.

Your mind is like an old house that needs to be renovated, but you cannot renovate it all at once. You must rebuild it one room, one thought, and one belief system at a time.

This is not for immediate gratification, to feel good now, and go back to the same stinking thinking. Real transformation takes time and repetition. It requires a daily renewal of the mind.

Your heart has a default setting and a bent to believe from the past. The only way to change the default setting is to build something new.

SECTION 3: MIND RENEWAL

Change does not happen until you get rid of the old mind and take on the new.

Renewing your mind daily is the key to sustaining freedom. As we start the next section, let us pick up the sword of the Spirit as we learn to renew our minds daily.

Day 1

You Can Be Rid of Your Demons, But Then You Have to Destroy The Lies They Energized.

Renewing your mind is the key to transforming your life. This is why the Word of God emphasizes that we renew our minds daily.

I was unknowingly stuck in the area of renewing my mind for years. I would have powerful encounters of deliverance and healing, but then find myself back in repeated cycles of defeat because I had never dealt with the belief system attached to the issue.

I had to go back into the place the lies entered and begin to weed, reseed, and water the roots of that belief system.

This is a common issue because people may not know what to do after a freedom encounter or how to renew their minds.

They experience peace because they have an encounter with the kingdom of God and truth. Often, they leave with "all the feels," but then they must go back out into the world.

Jesus unapologetically put it this way in Matthew 10:34 (NKJV), saying, "I did not come to bring peace but a sword."

In other words, Jesus cared about the powerful encounter of deliverance and healing, but it wasn't His priority. Transformation was His priority.

Transformation requires us to be equipped with the sword of the Spirit, the weapon that empowers us to wage the good war in our minds.

In 1 Timothy 1:18 (NKJV), Paul says, "Wage the good warfare." This type of warfare refers to a military engagement, a strategic assault on a deadly opponent.

Why does he say that? Because renewing the mind is ineffective with natural weapons. We can't wage a military campaign employing human weapons to achieve our aims.

2 Corinthians 10:4 (TPT) says:

> Instead, our spiritual weapons are energized with divine power to effectively dismantle the defenses behind which people hide. We can demolish every deceptive fantasy that opposes God and break through every arrogant attitude that is raised up in defiance of the true knowledge of God.

We must take lies and violently cast them down. We pull down every argument and imagination that exalts itself against the knowledge of God. We demolish every high thing that puffs itself up and rebels against God's nature, and His promises. We bring every thought into captivity to the obedience of Christ.

It is crucial to be aggressive because the enemy doesn't care if you are having a difficult day. He uses every weakness to double down on his efforts.

Many people have attached their identity to lies. To reclaim their identity as God's sons and daughters, they must use their spiritual weapons to go to war against every lie and replace it with the truth.

The lie only exists to war against our identity. If the enemy can steal your identity, he can steal your destiny. His tactic is to undermine the assignment God has for you. It is important to recognize the lie, but even more important to recognize the truth.

It is not enough to reject lies and get out of the red; we must replace them with the truth to get into the black.

The caveat is that people must know the truth. Even demons know the Word of God. We cannot have more knowledge of social media algorithms, where false prophets preach victim mentality and powerlessness, than the Word of God.

What are the areas that you have struggled to maintain freedom? What are the areas that you have made an inner vow that you will always deal with this issue and cannot break free? It is time to break free by destroying that lie.

Prayer

Holy Spirit, I come to you today in complete surrender. I recognize that I have tolerated cycles of ungodly belief systems that are keeping me in perpetual cycles of defeat. Today, I repent of the agreement that I have made with this lie, and I bring it to the cross. I break my agreement with this lie. I know that you delight to set your truth deep in my spirit. Come into the hidden places of my heart where I have held the lie hostage, wash me with the truth of your Word, purify my conscience, and make me clean again. The places that I have been crushed will rejoice in your healing touch. Restore me back better, energized and vivacious, full of life, prosperity, power, and strength. In Jesus' name, Amen.

Key Scriptures

Matthew 10:34 (NKJV); 1 Timothy 1:18 (NKJV); 2 Corinthians 10:4 (TPT)

Day 2

What is Not Processed is Repressed.

Renewing the mind is a continual process of rebuilding belief systems.

Once you stop agreeing with the lie, you can start receiving God's love in areas where it was previously obstructed. This allows you to break free from the mental stronghold and begin reprogramming your old belief system. By doing so, you can start living as a royal son or daughter, empowered by your true identity.

A few years back, I was finally able to break free from the grip of rejection and manage to stay free. Although I had received deliverance from rejection multiple times before, the stronghold of rejection kept resurfacing and raising its ugly head.

I reached a point where my soul was so deprived that I could not feel grateful for anything. My heart was filled with rejection, bitterness, and grief. It was swollen, inflamed, and infected. I could not even recognize any wins because I was only looking at everything through the lens of a victim.

I was tired of experiencing setbacks, so I decided to seek guidance from a Christian counselor.

The counselor helped me to recognize how I was being held captive by the enemy through busyness, career changes, transitions through significant life events such as marriage, traumatic issues with family, a desire for perfectionism, and a lack of revelation on how to rest.

She explained that the suppressed emotions ultimately caused me to lose self-awareness, become reactive in my emotions, and eventually led to emotional exhaustion. As a result of not dealing with the belief system of rejection, I began to lose control as the rejection manifested, bringing all its associates: fear, anxiety, depression, and escapism.

The counselor helped me learn the process of taking inventory of my thoughts. When I started to take inventory of the thoughts in my mind, I realized that they were rooted in self-rejection. I constantly blamed myself for not being good enough and criticized myself harshly. This had been going on for a long time.

Rejection curses what God has blessed and made perfect with His love.

The lack of attention to my inner world had led to the manifestation of struggles in my outer world. It was no surprise that I was losing self-awareness and treating myself poorly. I didn't realize that I was feeding myself with lies and becoming the byproduct of my toxic thinking.

Have you ever thought that you talk to yourself more than anyone else? It is important to know that your thoughts matter!

I had to go back to my belief systems and realize that I am not responsible for the actions or sins of those who have hurt me. However, I am responsible for how their actions, sins, or trauma have impacted me. I had to face the reality of that pain and take responsibility.

Processing triggers or emotions in real time and acknowledging how they made me feel was something I learned to do. In fact, God gave us emotions as a gift to serve as crucial indicators that alert us to pain.

WHAT IS NOT PROCESSED IS REPRESSED.

I also learned to become aware of the pain or emotional trigger. Once I am aware, I identify whether the pain or emotional trigger is rooted in truth or deception. If the thoughts are authentic, honorable, admirable, beautiful, respectful, pure, holy, merciful, and kind, as the Bible describes in Philippians 4:8 (TPT), then they are based on truth.

Unfortunately, during that time, I realized that many of my thoughts were based on lies. To overcome this, I had to learn to reject those lies. However, simply rejecting the lies was not enough; I had to replace them with the truth. And the truth is *always* the Word of God.

I would write down the truth and continue to meditate on it until the old thought process was replaced with a new one. It took me six months to rebuild my belief system and overcome self-rejection, but it has been a lasting change.

It is so important to recognize things that are painful, submit them to God, and allow His presence to minister to that place.

A practical tip when feeling triggered is to recognize it is a trigger, take a deep breath, and process the emotion instead of acting on it immediately. If you cannot process in real time, make a mental note to set aside time to process it completely at a later time. My recommendation is to be intentional about processing it the same day.

Everyone has their own way of processing. I love to process on my drive home from work. Initially, I recall the thoughts of my day and try to identify anything that may have triggered me or caused emotional pain or distress. I then ask the Lord to reveal any such thing and release it to Him, asking the Holy Spirit to minister to me. I follow this up with a session of worship. I journal my thoughts when I get home or during my quiet time. This approach helps me process my emotions and triggers, rather than suppressing them. It has helped me live a life of total freedom and peace.

Perhaps as you read this, you may sense the Holy Spirit bringing to your attention a recurring pattern of defeat in your life. Take a moment to reflect on the belief system that is responsible for causing chaos and dysfunction in your life. It is time to slow down, take inventory, invite the Holy Spirit, and allow Him to transform that belief system.

Let us start by praying today.

Prayer

Holy Spirit, I invite you to come into the places of my heart where I have been operating from deception. Show me the places where I have rehearsed lies from the enemy. Help me see the strongholds in my mind. Help me to separate the lies from the truth by dividing it with your Word, the absolute truth. Help me to let go of the control of my emotions and process them through the finished work of the cross. I commit to the complete surrender of my thoughts and emotions to you. I renew my mind daily, aligning my thoughts with your truth. Impart to me the riches of the spirit of wisdom and revelation. Consume me with your presence, peace, and joy. I put my trust in you. In Jesus' name, Amen.

Key Scriptures

Philippians 4:8 (TPT)

Day 3

Don't Ever Let The Devil Bring Shame And Condemnation Where God is Bringing Awareness.

If there was an issue that I have ministered on repeatedly, it is the spirit of condemnation behind the lies, "Why can't I stop?", "What have I done to cause this?", or "It must be my fault because of (blank)."

Condemnation is the enemy of identity. Condemnation muffles the inexhaustible love from God, the Father, who will never reject you, forsake you, or allow you to perform your way into acceptance.

God never expects your perfection. He only delights in your progress, and that is what He chooses to see.

Pain and condemnation do not come from God. However, God can use painful situations to make you aware of your need for His presence.

The devil is quite the opposite. His mission is to bring a double dose of condemnation. He blames you, then you blame yourself or someone else, so you never actually take responsibility for the pain. His intent is to keep you in a perpetual state of addiction, defeat, and struggle.

His mission is to undermine who God is and who you are.

In the Garden of Eden in Genesis 3:1 (NIV), he employed this tactic to undermine who God was with Eve by placing a seed of doubt, asking, "Did God really say?"

In other words, "Can you really trust God?"

One seed of doubt and abdication of responsibility was responsible for the fall of mankind.

In Matthew 3:17 (NKJV), we see that when the Holy Spirit came upon Jesus after He was baptized by John the Baptist, the heavens opened, and God spoke, saying,

"This is My beloved Son, in whom I am well pleased."

In the very next chapter, when Jesus is in the wilderness being tempted by the devil, the devil's words to him in Matthew 4:3 (NKJV) were, "If you are the Son of God, command that these stones become bread."

This was the attempt to undermine the identity of who Jesus was. Jesus overcame because He didn't allow the condemnation from the devil to compromise His identity.

Romans 8:1 (TPT) says:

> So *now the case is closed*. There remains no accusing voice of condemnation against those who are joined in life-union with Jesus, the Anointed One.

Continuing in verse 3:

> God sent us his Son in human form to identify with human weakness. Clothed with humanity, God's Son gave his body to be the sin-offering so that God could once and for all condemn the guilt and power of sin.

Finally, in verse 5, it finishes, saying:

Those who are motivated by the flesh only pursue what benefits themselves. But those who live by the impulses of the Holy Spirit are motivated to pursue spiritual realities. For the sense and reason of the flesh is death, but the mind-set controlled by the Spirit finds life and peace. In fact, the mind-set focused on the flesh fights God's plan and refuses to submit to His direction, because it cannot!

Remember, you are God's own. He already knew everything about you before your beginning. Knowing that, He chose you. He was willing to take a risk on you. He sent His most precious son, Jesus, to take all your shame and condemnation so that you can be redeemed. In return, He only desires to be in the right relationship with His kids. His goodness and mercy lead us to repentance, dismantling strongholds of shame and condemnation so that we can put on the mind of Christ.

Where have you found yourself identifying with the problem or issue instead of who you are in Christ?

Prayer

Heavenly Father, I repent for my agreement with condemnation and shame. I repent for not taking responsibility for the pain, blaming myself or others, and not allowing the Holy Spirit into my struggle. I renounce every agreement I have made with shame and condemnation. I capture, like prisoners of war, every thought and insist that it bow in obedience to the Anointed One. I declare that I am the righteousness of God in Christ Jesus, and therefore, there is no condemnation for me because I abide in Christ Jesus. Let me passionately pursue a new way of thinking according to your truth and seeing myself through the finished work of the cross. Thank you for restoring my identity and restoring me back into the right relationship with you. In Jesus' name, Amen.

Key Scriptures

Genesis 3:1 (NIV); Matthew 3:17 (NKJV); Matthew 4:3 (NKJV); Romans 8:1, 3, 5–7 (TPT)

Day 4

God Doesn't Re-Create; He Only Creates. Anytime You Try to Re-create Your Life, You Are Living Under The Wrong Influence.

Remember, the devil doesn't create; he imitates.

You cannot create a future if you continue to re-create the past.

Isaiah 43:18–19 (NKJV) says:

> Do not remember the former things, Nor consider the things of old. Behold, I will do a new thing, Now it shall spring forth; Shall you not know it?

Many people remain stuck because they are still re-creating from past experiences, both successes and failures, and bringing them into the present.

They want God to bless their plans, but are they *His* plans? Are those plans just for God, or are they with God?

Re-creating the past will cause you to be a slave to fear and limitation. It keeps you from stepping out to do the new thing.

Where have you been trying to put old wine into new wineskins and becoming frustrated when it does not work out?

Did that business idea fail after all the time and investment? *Create* something new!

Were you believing for a spouse, but that relationship did not work out? *Create* a new plan.

Did not get pregnant the first time you tried? *Create* again!

Don't keep doing the same thing expecting a different result. Step out!

Did that investment or real estate property not work out? Step out again with the wisdom you gained, get a team of experts in those areas, and *create* a new strategy.

Tired of sowing seed and not receiving the harvest? It may be time to take it up a level, sow a sacrificial offering, bless someone in need, or honor someone who has what you have been believing for! *Create* the life you want to live!

You know that you are healed once you stop dwelling on your past and start adopting the mindset of Christ.

You must speak to your mind, will, and emotions.

I have had situations come where memories from the past are triggered and I need to manage my thoughts and emotions.

In those moments, I must speak to my mind, will, and emotions by literally saying, "No, you will not expect the worst; you will only expect the best."

I must command my soul and tell it what to do. To do that, you must reprogram the space between your right and left ear.

Mark Twain said, "I've been through many hard things in my life, some that actually happened."

We do not need to create monsters in our minds. Instead, we should take control of our thoughts, making them obedient to the resurrection power of Jesus' finished work on the cross.

GOD DOESN'T RE-CREATE; HE ONLY CREATES ... 83

Transforming our lives is a continuous process, and it starts with renewing our minds every single day. As Romans 12:2 (NKJV) aptly puts it, "Be transformed by the renewing of your mind."

This is one of the best ways to be empowered to discern God's will, His plan, and His purpose for you.

So, let us make a commitment to renew our minds daily, and watch as our lives are gradually transformed for the better.

What thoughts do you need to write down and attack with a declaration or a scripture?

Here are two simple declarations:

I am the righteousness of God in Christ Jesus. (2 Corinthians 5:21, NLT)

There is therefore now no condemnation for those who are in Christ Jesus. (Romans 8:1, ESV)

Prayer

Lord, I come to you today with this ungodly mindset I have been experiencing. I take this thought captive by violently pulling it down and making it obedient to Jesus. I demolish every deceptive fantasy that opposes the Word of God and any thought that elevates itself against the true knowledge of God. I replace it with the infallible Word of God, which is the absolute, unrivaled truth. I stand in complete victory and exercise my authority over this area of my life. Thank you, Jesus, for the resurrection power that gives me the faith to overcome. In Jesus' name, Amen.

Key Scriptures

Isaiah 43:18–19 (NKJV); Romans 12:2 (NKJV); 2 Corinthians 5:21 (NLT); Romans 8:1 (ESV)

Day 5

Renewing Your Mind Will Transform Your Life, But No One Can Renew Your Mind But You.

The path toward healing is a lifelong journey that requires unwavering dedication and commitment. Venturing down this narrow road can be daunting, but it is the path less traveled that often leads to the most rewarding experiences.

Joshua 1:8 (TPT) gives clear instruction from God:

> Recite this scroll of the law constantly. Contemplate it day and night and be careful to follow every word it contains; then you will enjoy incredible prosperity and success.

Many people desire the prosperity and success of others, yet they are unwilling to pay the price of meditating and focusing on God's Word until it transforms them.

When we rehearse and recite the Word of God, we enlist in the war against the strategies of the accuser.

Ephesians 6:12–18 (TPT) says:

> Your hand-to-hand combat is not with human beings, but with the highest principalities and authorities operating in rebellion under the heavenly realms. For they are a powerful class of demon-gods and evil spirits that hold this dark world in bondage.

Because of this, you must wear all the armor that God provides so you're protected as you confront the slanderer, for you are destined for all things and will rise victorious. Put on truth as a belt to strengthen you to stand in triumph. Put on holiness as the protective armor that covers your heart. Stand on your feet alert, then you'll always be ready to share the blessings of peace. In every battle, take faith as your wrap-around shield, for it is able to extinguish the blazing arrows coming at you from the evil one! Embrace the power of salvation's full deliverance, like a helmet to *protect your thoughts from lies*. And take the mighty razor-sharp Spirit-sword of the spoken word of God.

The enemy loves to distract, sidetrack, and disrupt your mind through chaotic thinking. You must make the choice to pick up the right weapons and fight the right fight.

The enemy will always send every kind of lie to undermine the Word of God, the nature of God, and the character of God. He uses intimidation to try to lure you into changing your position and your authority in Christ.

So, the weapons God gives us are not to defend ourselves against the devil, but to destroy him in the name of the one whose power is limitless and above every kingdom.

I don't wait for a season of test and trial to use the weapons given to me through Ephesians 6. The two I use most frequently are the shield of faith and the sword of the Spirit.

I use the shield of faith to catch, block, and extinguish every fiery dart (lie) of the enemy. My faith absorbs the illegal thoughts and suggestions from the enemy.

If an arrow, or lie, happens to get past that shield of faith, I use the sword of the Spirit to dig out the lie and replace it with the truth.

I use the shield of faith to block lies, but I use the sword of the Spirit, the Word of God, to destroy them.

Your thoughts have the power to shape your reality. If you empower the lie, you empower the liar. Lies require more lies to be sustained. On the other hand, when you empower the truth, you disempower the lie. The truth has all of heaven behind it; the lie has nothing behind it but to undermine the truth. Therefore, it is important to choose your thoughts and beliefs wisely, as they can either empower you or disempower you.

Our response to the process of healing determines the outcome. Do we meditate and dwell on evil, illegitimate thoughts, creating a dwelling place for the enemy to live unrecognized? Do we live in opposition to who God says we really are? Or do we meditate and wield the weapon of the Word of God, elevating it above every thought, and believe God's Word above every circumstance?

Let us choose the path of strength and victory by choosing to believe in and wield the power of God's Word. Only then, God's Word becomes our reality; everything else is imagination.

The renewal of the mind is what makes the miraculous possible in people's lives because you have the mind of Christ. Our belief system is now rooted in what God sees and what He says. When our sight is restored, we have vision, and with God, we can create the life that we are meant to live.

Now the lie that worked against you will work for you because you used the Word of God to build up your faith, which will lend itself to the miraculous.

What areas have you become passive in your devotion and meditation on scriptures? Where have you empowered the lie instead of the Word of God? Is there a deficit in an area of your life where there should be abundance?

Prayer

Lord, I come to you and confess that I have been distracted by the voices of the world instead of the truth and the knowledge that can only come from abiding in your Word. I come into alignment and agreement with the promises and the truth of the living Word. I take these weapons that I have been given, and I pray that you supernaturally infuse me with strength through my union with you. I stand victorious with the force of your explosive power flowing in and through me. I put on this complete set of armor that you have provided for me so that I can be protected as I fight against the evil strategies of the accuser. The battle was won over 2,000 years ago, so I position myself from the place of victory, and let your blood avenge and assault every weapon that attempts to form against my mind and my future. Thank you for blessing me with every blessing in the heavenly realm. I choose to think and live from that place. In Jesus' name, Amen.

Key Scriptures

Joshua 1:8 (TPT); Ephesians 6:12–18 (TPT)

Section 4

Prayer

The outcome of prayer should always be transformation because prayer is meant to be an exchange. Pray until you become the prayer itself.

"Though I love them, they stand accusing me like Satan for what I've never done. I will pray until I become prayer itself."

Psalms 109:4, TPT

This is a compelling statement David makes in Psalm 109:4.

The outcome of effective prayer is transformation. Have you become the person who can properly steward the outcome of your prayer?

Your biggest platform of influence is your secret place.

To pray is to give yourself fully to God. When was the last time you became the product of your prayers?

Are we bringing God a list of demands, or are we giving Him ourselves?

I am not saying our ask isn't important; it is *so* important. However, if our ask is the only way we approach prayer, we have missed the intended purpose.

Giving ourselves to God opens us up to incredible transformation. We take on His divine nature, which leads to a profound change within us. This exchange with God is powerful and life-changing, and it is available to anyone willing to surrender themselves to Him.

Are you confused about your life? Pray.

Are you tired of being stuck? Pray.

Do you want to see the vision come to pass? Pray.

Are you still waiting for an answer? Pray.

Do you need to figure out what to do next in a given situation? Pray.

Are you questioning God's Word, His nature, and His character? Pray.

We pray until we become the prayer because God hasn't changed, and He won't change. But sometimes, our circumstances only change once we do. Can I encourage you not to look at prayer as "doing" but instead as a state of "being"?

The level of communion and intimacy we build with God in the secret place through prayer greatly determines the outcome of our lives.

In the words of Charles Spurgeon:

> The power of prayer can never be overrated. If a man can but pray he can do anything. He who knows how to overcome with God in prayer has Heaven and earth at his disposal.

Let us embark on a journey to discover the life-changing power of prayer as we seek to commune with God over the next five days.

Day 1

As God's Kids, We Don't Have to Pray, "If It's God's Will." We Know Him, So We Pray His Will.

I wonder how many prayers stay in delay or never come to fruition because of lack of revelation and application of Matthew 6:8–10 (NKJV):

> For your Father knows the things you have need of before you ask Him. In this manner, therefore, pray: Our Father in heaven, Hallowed be Your name. Your kingdom come. Your will be done On earth as it is in heaven.

For instance, when we pray for healing, we don't have to pray, "If it's your will, Lord, heal them," because God doesn't cause sickness. In fact, it is His will that *all* should be healed. Knowing the truth, we lay hands on the sick and command sickness to go, and God's will is that they *will* recover.

If God instructs you to go into a territory and take it, you don't have to pray, "If it's His will for me to buy that house or purchase that building, I will purchase it." Instead, you pray His providence, trusting that He will go before you and make a way because His will is His promises fulfilled.

I believe ineffective prayers stem from a lack of divine revelation that is completely accessible to those willing to receive. God has already taught us how to pray; His will is His Word. The more we know His Word, the more we know Him, and we pray accordingly.

When people learn not to permit things on Earth that do not exist in Heaven, they do not react in fear or allow timidity to muffle God's voice. Instead, they learn how to pray. Then the voice of faith rises and becomes the loudest and most compelling voice.

One of my favorite illustrations of this is the story of Hannah in 1 Samuel 1 (NKJV). The Bible speaks of a man named Elkinah, a man who had two wives. One was Peninnah, who Elkinah favored less, but she could bear children. The other was Hannah, who Elkinah favored more, but the Bible says that "the Lord had closed her womb."

What is most interesting about Hannah is that in her time, a woman's worth was measured by her ability to have children, but Hannah was unable to conceive. Despite her circumstances, Hannah was a woman of faith because Hannah was a woman of prayer.

There were days where Hannah was provoked and mocked by the other wife, aka fertile-myrtle Peninnah. There were days where Hannah was accused of being drunk because she prayed so passionately.

Even in the face of accusations, injustice, and pain, she faithfully showed up to the temple to pray because God had given her His word for a son of promise. So, Hannah took that promise and brought her outside circumstances into her inside secret place. As she prayed, she began to develop intimacy with God. Even though the culture of the world surrounded her, she had the culture of the kingdom within her.

See, Hannah made her secret place a priority. The Bible says for many years Hannah showed up to her secret place every day without fail, even on the days she felt disheartened and grieved.

She did not limit her connection with God to her own terms. In other words, she didn't lower God's words and His promises down to the level of her experience. Instead, she brought her experience up to the level of God's Word.

Finally, the day came where Elkinah knew his wife, Hannah, and the Bible says, the Lord remembered her prayer.

In Samuel 1:20 (AMP), it says:

> It came about in due time, after Hannah had conceived, that she gave birth to a son; she named him Samuel, saying, "Because I have asked for him from the Lord."

Later, we find that God didn't open her womb once, but she gave birth to three sons and two daughters because God always finishes what He starts.

The years she prayed in faith were preparing the next generation for a Samuel. Samuel anointed the first kings, delivered the Word of the Lord in a day that it was rare, was appointed and anointed as a prophet of the Lord. Samuel brought the prophetic voice into the next generation, and his words were never unfulfilled.

Hannah saved what could have potentially been an extinct generation in her prayer closet.

What prayers do you need to pray to ignite faith and belief to see God's promises fulfilled? Whose future is on the other side of your faith-filled petition?

Prayer

Jesus, I come into agreement with what the Word of God says about my situation. Even though man and circumstances may attempt to have the first say, your Word will get the final say. I thank you that you watch over your Word to perform it. Not a single word from you is empty of power.

Not a single word that comes from you will ever fall to the ground. I stand in the authority of God's Word, and I speak to the mountain of my situation and declare it be removed. Every mountain shall be made low, and every valley shall be exalted. I declare the rough places shall be made smooth and the crooked places shall become straight. Let the outcome of my prayer bring you glory and let me be a witness to others. I thank you that all your promises are YES and AMEN. In Jesus' name, Amen.

Key Scriptures

Matthew 6:8–10 (NKJV); 1 Samuel 1:5 (NKJV); 1 Samuel 1:20 (AMP)

Day 2

Dark Seasons Should Never Dim Your Light; They Should Make Your Light Brighter.

One morning, I woke up with a particular thought and scripture.

The title of Proverbs 31 in the TPT is "The Radiant Bride." This isn't a chapter about the perfect woman as much as it is a chapter about the bride of Christ walking in her true identity.

Proverbs 31:17–18 (TPT) says:

> She wraps herself in strength, might, and power in all her works. She tastes and experiences a better substance, and her shining light will not be extinguished, no matter how dark the night.

In other words, even in the dark season, she is anointed with power to do the works of Jesus.

Her prayer life is the light that overcomes her circumstances even in a culture or, seemingly, a season where darkness prevails.

Her light shines brighter with every winter that she overcomes.

Looking for a prophecy? Here is one from Isaiah 60:1–5 (AMP):

> Arise [from spiritual depression to a new life], shine [be radiant with the glory and brilliance of the Lord]; for your light has come, And the glory and brilliance of the Lord has risen upon you. For

in fact, darkness will cover the earth And deep darkness will cover the peoples; But the Lord will rise upon you [Jerusalem] And His glory and brilliance will be seen on you. Nations will come to your light, And kings to the brightness of your rising. Lift up your eyes around you and see; They all gather together, they come to you. Your sons will come from far away, And your daughters will be looked after at *their* side. Then you will see and be radiant, And your heart will tremble [with joy] and rejoice Because the abundant wealth of the seas will be brought to you, The wealth of the nations will come to you.

Sometimes, life can seem muddy, cloudy, and confusing. Sometimes, in our flesh, we can become disoriented by the cares of life and delayed breakthroughs.

Here's a tip: Be quiet. Sit still before the Lord and train yourself to wait on Him. When you allow your heart to be still, God's voice can penetrate.

David, a man after God's own heart, speaks of this over and over.

Psalms 4:3–4 (TPT) says this:

> May we never forget that YAHWEH works wonders for every one of his devoted lovers. And this is how I know that he will answer my every prayer. Tremble in awe before the Lord, and do not sin against him. Be still upon your bed and search your heart before him.

In Psalms 46:10 (NKJV), it says, "Be still and know that I am God."

Exodus 14:14 (NIV) declares, "The Lord will fight for you; you need only to be still."

Can you have a quiet voice and a still heart? God wants to be the first to speak into your day, but He will not compete with your voice or any other.

Let every circumstance be an opportunity to wait on the Lord and pray until the breakthrough comes.

Don't ever waste a dark season or a wilderness. It is there where you dig the wells. It is there where you become more deeply dependent on Jesus. It is there where you purchase the most precious oil that does not run out, burn out, but instead, goes the distance.

What areas of your life have you let your flame flicker instead of putting fresh oil on the wick so your light can shine brighter? What problems do you need to turn into prayers?

Prayer

Holy Spirit, I ask you to shine the light on the dim places of my heart. Expose the areas where the light is flickering out. Where are the places that have lost translucence? Open every window of my heart and let the light in. Let your anointing come and lubricate my lamp again so that I can emerge out of darkness and become the light the world needs. Turn my prayers of worry over problems into strategies and solutions. I surrender this season to you. In Jesus' name, Amen.

Key Scriptures

Proverbs 31:17–18 (TPT); Isaiah 60:1–5 (AMP); Psalms 4:3–4 (TPT); Psalms 46:10 (NKJV); Exodus 14:14 (NIV)

Day 3

The Purpose of Prayer is Not For God to Take Away Your Problems; The Purpose of Prayer is to Produce The Power to Overcome.

Are you asking God for more revelation, more kingdom strategies, and the manifestation of miracles?

The answer often comes through a problem, a "thorn in the side."

If you can surrender the thorn, problem, or pain, it will become a portal for God's power.

Instead of idolizing a problem, weaponize it in prayer. Turn those prayers into praise and gaze at Jesus.

A prayer of praise defeats the enemy you cannot defeat with your own strength.

You will be transformed to the level you gaze at Jesus. When you appeal to His character, then you will see His provision.

I love the way Paul, who wrote most of the New Testament, puts it in 2 Corinthians 12:7–10 (TPT):

> The extraordinary level of the revelations I've received is no reason for anyone to exalt me. For this is why a thorn in my flesh was given to me, the Adversary's messenger sent to harass me, keeping me from becoming arrogant. Three times I pleaded

with the Lord to relieve me of this. But he answered me, "My grace is always more than enough for you, and my power finds its full expression through your weakness." So, I will celebrate my weaknesses, for when I'm weak I sense more deeply the mighty power of Christ living in me. So I'm not defeated by my weakness, but delighted! For when I feel my weakness and endure mistreatment—when I'm surrounded with troubles on every side and face persecution because of *my love* for Christ—I am made yet stronger. For my weakness becomes a portal to God's power.

Paul expresses the importance of being vulnerable with painful situations, especially in the position of leadership.

Vulnerability means "wound possibility," a greater probability of being hurt.

Sometimes, to lead and have a greater influence for the kingdom, we must take risks, including the possibility of being hurt by others or the circumstances of life.

Personally, I have been through many deeply painful circumstances in my life, but I learn from each situation. The most valuable lesson I have learned is instead of repressing pain, I express it before the Lord on my knees. I process my pain in prayer.

In prayer, the pain that was meant to crush me now takes me to a pleasant place, a pasture place. I come out of those seasons feeling more deeply loved and connected to God. I have found a joy in Him I wouldn't have if I didn't experience that pain.

Psalms 23:1–5 (TPT) is the perfect template for prayer:

> YAHWEH is my best friend and my shepherd. I always have more than enough. He offers a resting place for me in his luxurious love. His tracks take me to an oasis of peace near the

quiet brook of bliss. That's where he restores and revives my life. He opens before me the right path and leads me along in his footsteps of righteousness so that I can bring honor to his name. Even when your path takes me through the valley of deepest darkness, fear will never conquer me, for you already have! Your authority is my strength and my peace. The comfort of your love takes away my fear. I'll never be lonely, for you are near. You become my delicious feast even when my enemies dare to fight. You anoint me with the fragrance of your Holy Spirit; you give me all I can drink of you until my cup overflows.

Prayer

Lord, I bow my knees in complete surrender to you. I give my pain to you on this altar as an act of worship. I acknowledge that you bore all my grief and pain so that I do not have to bear burdens that you have already lifted. I recognize the pain that this has caused, and Holy Spirit, I ask that you come into this place with me. Bring me comfort and supernatural healing. I refuse to seek comfort in other things and to conceal the pain that needs to be brought into the open. In deep dependency, I give you my pain in exchange for your power; let it come rest upon me. In Jesus' name, Amen.

Key Scriptures

2 Corinthians 12:7–10 (TPT); Psalms 23:1–5 (TPT)

Day 4

Sometimes, We Need to Go Without Bread to Get a Word From God. But God Doesn't Want You to Give Up Bread as Much as He Wants You to Give Up Distraction.

Matthew 4:4 (NKJV) says, "Man shall not live by bread alone, but by every word that proceeds from the mouth of God."

When we study Jesus' life, we see that He made it a normal routine to separate Himself to pray.

Mark 1:35 (TPT) says, "Jesus got up long before daylight, left the house while it was dark, and made his way to a secluded place to give himself to prayer."

Jesus would position Himself in prayer before ministering to anyone, showing His discipline and dedication.

Although Jesus did not lack self-control, there was no temptation to wake up to scroll a screen or show up to post on a social media platform before He showed up to post in His secret place.

God's love language is quality time, and He is a jealous God, but He is not going to beg for our attention.

This is why devoting ourselves to prayer and fasting is so powerful. Fasting is not a works-based, religious performance meant for the public space. Fasting is sacrificial prayer in the secret place that builds intimacy with God and moves His heart.

In Mark Chapter 9:14–29 (TPT), Jesus met a man who asked for help healing his son. This man was angry that Jesus' disciples could not do it. His son had a "mute spirit" since birth, most likely a generational curse. When the spirit seized him, it would throw him down to the ground; he would gnash his teeth and foam at the mouth.

This boy had a stubborn problem that was resistant to change, but the mute spirit that seized him wasn't the problem.

Jesus said to the crowd, "Why are you such a faithless people? How much longer must I remain with you and put up with your unbelief? Now, bring the boy to me."

They brought the boy to Jesus, and as soon as the demon saw Jesus, it started manifesting. The boy's father asked Jesus to do something.

In response, Jesus said, "If you are able to believe (get rid of your unbelief), all things are possible to the believer."

The boy's father cried out, "I do believe, Lord; help my little faith!"

Jesus helped this man recognize and become aware of the problem. It was his own unbelief.

Immediately, Jesus rebuked the demon, saying, "Deaf and mute spirit, I command you to come out of him!"

The demon came out, then Jesus took the boy's hand and helped him up. The boy was completely set free from a problem that had plagued him since birth.

When Jesus' disciples asked Him why they could not perform the miracle, He answered them, saying, "This type of powerful spirit can only be cast out by fasting and prayer."

I believe Jesus used this particular example to reveal that just as there was a physical relationship between the boy with the deaf and mute spirit, and the father with the spirit of unbelief, there is a spiritual relationship between the inability to hear the voice of God and speak His Word (remember, faith comes by hearing and hearing by the Word of God) and a spirit of unbelief.

The breakthrough for this boy's instant healing was made possible through the breaking of his father's unbelief.

Personally, I can attest that I never knew what I didn't have faith for until I fasted. I never knew how much unbelief had sometimes been hidden in my flesh until I fasted. I didn't know what I didn't know. It wasn't until I got myself in a place where I could hear the voice of God, receive the Word of God, and declare the Word of God those things shifted and breakthroughs came.

You cannot come into union with God and build intimacy with Him and still live in unbelief.

What areas do you see stubborn, resistant problems that have led to disillusion and unbelief? Have you allowed the distractions and the cares of life to steal the seed of God's Word and His promises?

Pray this prayer over yourself today.

Prayer

In Jesus' name, I cancel and terminate every thought, image, or picture of failure concerning impossible situations. I loosen the grip of every spirit of doubt and unbelief in my heart. Let the angels of the Living God roll away every stone of hindrance to the manifestation of breakthroughs. Every opposition standing in the way of my breakthrough, I command you to move by fire in Jesus' name. I command every stubborn problem to come out with all your roots. I release turnaround breakthroughs.

I release the spirit of faith. I release the acceleration of miracles in the mighty and matchless name of Jesus, Amen.

Key Scriptures

Matthew 4:4 (NKJV); Mark 1:35 (TPT); Mark 9:14–29 (TPT)

Day 5

Perhaps Prayers For Breakthrough Are Not About Waiting For God to Move Us as Much as They Are About Praying In Such A Way That Our Prayers Move Him.

God does not respond to need; He responds to faith. Anyone can bring a list of needs to God, but God wants us to pray for the impossible. The size and magnitude of your prayers are a reflection of the size and magnitude of your faith.

In Ezekiel 22 (TPT), God deals with a nation much like we see in the world today. Israel had turned away from Him and lent themselves to idolatry, human sacrifice, false prophets, and oppression of the vulnerable. Jerusalem had become a bloody city, stained and defiled by her own sins.

In Ezekiel 22:30, the Lord speaks a sobering word to the prophet Ezekiel:

> I searched for someone who would repair the wall, one who fills the gap, an intercessor to cry out for mercy, but I found no one. There was no one found who would keep my justice from destroying the nation.

In those days, God appointed prophets to be watchmen. If the prophet was not obedient to speak the Word of the Lord, the blood would be on the prophet's hands.

Ezekiel had to intercede and deliver unpopular truths to the nation about the consequences of their sins. He commissioned the wicked to repent from their evil ways, change their thinking, and return to righteousness, then their lives would be spared.

Sometimes, God requires us to do hard things, but He is looking for just one who will be faithful and go against the current.

In the first chapter of the book of Daniel in the Old Testament, we see young Daniel, a prophet, interpreter of dreams and visions, commissioned to serve King Nebuchadnezzar in his palace.

At an early age, Daniel refused to defile himself with the king's food because it had been previously offered to idols. He asked to be tested for ten days. He fasted alongside three other servants, eating only vegetables and water for ten days.

After the testing, he and the servants were better in appearance and fatter in flesh than all the youths who ate the king's food. God gave them learning and skill in all literature and wisdom, and Daniel had understanding in all vision and dreams. Furthermore, in every matter of wisdom and understanding that the king inquired of them, the king found them ten times better than all the magicians and enchanters in his kingdom.

Daniel continued to interpret dreams and visions, gained favor with the king, and received promotions for several years.

Later in Daniel 6 (AMP), the Bible says that Daniel began serving King Darius as a chief commissioner and was distinguished because of his excellent spirit. The commissioners sought to find fault in him but failed because of his integrity. So, they looked for a basis to accuse him through his connection with God.

They convinced King Darius to sign an injunction that anyone who prays to any god or man besides the king for a period of thirty days would be thrown into the den of lions.

When Daniel heard about the document, his response was to go into his house and open his windows so that he could be seen in clear view. He proceeded to get down on his knees three times a day to pray and give thanks. When the commissioners found him, he was interceding, making his petitions known to God.

The king favored Daniel, so he was very reluctant to command Daniel to be brought down and thrown into the den of lions. So, as he moved forward, he said in verse 16, "May your God, whom you constantly serve, rescue you Himself!"

Even the king fasted all night. When he came to the den in the morning, Daniel spoke triumphantly in verse 21, "O king, live forever! My God has sent His angel and has shut the mouths of the lions so that they have not hurt me, because I was found innocent before Him; and also before you, O king, I have committed no crime."

Daniel was set free and found without injury. Furthermore, the king had all of Daniel's accusers, their wives, and children thrown into the den of lions. Then, the king issued a decree that men will reverently fear and tremble before the God of Daniel!

It was Daniel's lifestyle of steadfast faith and devotion to prayer that gave him the courage and tenacity to live in such a way that he was found innocent in the courts of Heaven and the courts on Earth. His testing, fasting, and persistent prayers were the prerequisite to overcoming the den of lions, causing the nation to turn away from compromise and turn back to fear and reverence of the Lord.

In 2021, COVID vaccine mandates were given to healthcare workers and many professionals nationwide. Most people were given a grace period to present a religious exemption, but there were many stipulations. Many healthcare workers and professionals were in fear their exemptions would be rejected and they would lose their employment. Many had to support their families and were overcome with anxiety and stress.

The Lord commissioned me to start a prayer meeting and, essentially, an awareness campaign on social media that would empower people to pray effectively, fervently and intercede on behalf of those who were at risk of unemployment. Through prayer, we believed that we would receive God-given wisdom and strategy on how to present our arguments to our employers.

I was used to prayer meetings in a spirit-filled, apostolic church, where prayers were pregnant with faith, but going to the marketplace would be a great challenge because many people operated in fear. The Lord was asking me to go change the thermostat to faith, equip people to pray in power, believe, and then to act on their prayers.

This was like having a second job. I had to make Instagram posts, as well as answer a plethora of direct messages and emails after a long workday. Every Wednesday, I got up at 5:00 a.m. and hosted a live prayer meeting for healthcare workers.

Initially, it started locally. Then people began to join from other parts of California, other states, and other nations.

We began to cry out, petition and declare. We began to speak the things that weren't as though they were. We turned the voice of fear down and the voice of faith up. We prophesied the outcome of the mandates would rule in our favor.

These prayer meetings and daily social media engagements went on for months, but there came a day that these religious exemptions were accepted. Testimonies rolled in of people who had been able to keep their jobs and everyone who persisted in prayer came out better. In fact, even today I continue to receive testimonials from men and women who have said that if it wasn't for the wisdom they gained, they wouldn't have been able to confront their employers and would have lost their jobs.

God was looking for one woman that would be a watchman like the prophet Ezekiel and be obedient to speak and carry out His word. He was looking for one who would stand in the gap, expose the evil, and show others how to win the present battle and every future battle ahead.

He was looking for a woman who, like Daniel, would not bow her knee to the little gods of government and would empower others to do the same. As a result, hundreds of healthcare workers were restored back to employment.

God didn't respond to our need for jobs; He responded to our faith. It was a movement that didn't just change my family, but many families.

What areas of your life has God called you to be a watchman, to stand in the gap and move His heart for a person or a situation? Is there a situation or person your heart burns for in your city, your neighborhood, or in your family? Are there areas God is calling you to be brave and courageous?

Don't let the enemy steal your voice at the point of prayer. Rise up, pray, and act. God will always reward faithfulness, obedience, and courage.

Prayer

Lord, I come to you and confess that I have been complacent and silent in the area that you have called me to stand in the gap. I repent for letting fear and intimidation steal my voice. In obedience, I rise in the office of my divine assignment, and I petition heaven to open over my city, community, and family. I pray that the Father of Glory will unveil within me the unlimited riches of His glory and favor until supernatural strength fills my innermost being with divine might and explosive power. I will never doubt your mighty power to work in me to accomplish more than my greatest request and my most unbelievable dreams. Your miraculous power constantly energizes me. In Jesus' name, Amen.

Key Scriptures

Ezekiel 22:30 (TPT); Daniel 6:16, 21 (AMP)

Section 5

Fear of the Lord

God will not always deliver you out, but He will lead you through.

"And you shall remember that the Lord your God led you all the way these forty years in the wilderness, to humble you and test you, to know what was in your heart, whether you would keep His commandments or not. So He humbled you, allowed you to hunger, and fed you with manna which you did not know nor did your fathers know, that He might make you know that man shall not live by bread alone; but man lives by every word that proceeds from the mouth of the Lord."

Deuteronomy 8:2–3, NKJV

There are times when God does not deliver or rescue us from a circumstance or a season, but we can be guaranteed that He will lead us through.

If we don't trust God in the negative, we can't be trustworthy in the positive.

Bill Johnson puts it this way:

> Sometimes God will lead you through so that He can put the weight of His glory on you. That weight establishes a sanctified life but crushes an unsanctified life. God measures what we can carry without it breaking what He was building.

God wants to lead us to pray in faith so we respond with authority.

Adverse winds in life may shake us and break us, but they are meant to make us.

People living as slaves will beg God to deliver them out, but people living as sons and daughters will allow God to lead them through.

From a personal standpoint, I have navigated the adverse winds of life in a perfectly imperfect way. However, I have allowed the challenges of difficult times and adversity to lead me to my knees, come to the end of myself, become less self-reliant and more intimate.

Adversity gives God the opportunity to prepare us for something bigger that we may not fully understand, and it requires a quiet and confident trust.

2 Timothy 1:12-14 (TPT) is so encouraging:

> The confidence of my calling enables me to overcome every difficulty without shame, for I have an intimate revelation of this God. And my faith in him convinces me that he is more

than able to keep all that I've placed in his hands safe and secure until the fullness of his appearing. Allow the healing words you've heard from me to live in you and make them a model for life as your faith and love for the Anointed One *grows even more*. Guard well this incomparable treasure by the Spirit of Holiness living within you.

As we start the next section, my prayer is that you will step into a deeper reverence and awe for God, that you will turn away from sin, and that you will develop a complete trust and dependence in God in every circumstance.

Day 1

Once You See Jesus For Who He Is, You Will Never Live Your Life a Slave to The Substitute.

I receive communion almost every day in my home. I do not do this as a religious duty, but I recognize it is a holy moment to sit and share a meal with Jesus.

In Luke 22:15 (NLT), the Bible says that Jesus was eager to eat this Passover meal with His disciples prior to His crucifixion.

This really shows how relational Jesus was. Even in His last moments, He invited His disciples to receive this meal. They didn't have to earn their place at this table because we do not give communion, we receive it.

Jesus wasn't transactional. If He was transactional, Judas, His betrayer, would never have been invited, and none of us would qualify.

By having this revelation, when I receive communion, I don't approach this moment by taking emblems and checking a box. Communion is about the King of Glory inviting us to sit with Him at His table where He serves Himself as the main course.

He wants us to know Him intimately. When you know Him, you can see Him for who He really is. Many people live defeated, counterfeit lives because they do not know Him.

So, Jesus said to receive this meal often because He knows that once we taste of the real thing, we will never have to live our lives a slave to the substitutions, the little gods. When we know Him, we know the power of His resurrection.

I know this because when I lost my dad to suicide in 2023, it was the most painful trial I have ever walked through. During that time, I decided that if I was going to go through this kind of pain, I didn't want any substitutions. I only wanted Jesus.

I found myself with Him at this table day after day. I will tell you, as I knew Him on a deeper level, He took all the grief and pain. However, these were not the only things that left. Every stronghold, old mindset, and any part of my flesh that no longer served me was crucified.

We know from Jesus' example, when things die, they get resurrected. He didn't raise me back to normal; He raised me back to new because He is the resurrection and the life. He came to bring life and life more abundantly. I was resurrected to a new person: more authentic, more compassionate, and more loving toward people.

I invite you to take communion with me today. Let us accept this life-giving invitation today as we receive.

Prayer

Lord, we ask that you examine our hearts and reveal the places that keep us from knowing you. As we receive your body and your blood, we thank you for the provision that you have already made for our freedom. We declare that as we receive you, Jesus, sickness will die, and healing will be resurrected. We declare captivity will be crucified, and liberty will be resurrected. We declare poverty will die, and prosperity will be resurrected. Barrenness will die, and fruitfulness will be resurrected. May our lives be an illustration of the same power that raised Christ

Jesus from the dead and elevated Him to the highest place of authority and power. In Jesus' name, Amen.

Key Scriptures

Luke 22:15 (NLT)

Day 2

I Would Rather Use a Wilderness Season as a Training Ground For Future Battles Than Stay Stuck as a Consequence of Complacency.

Wilderness avoidance is war avoidance. The wilderness was meant to train us for war. Sadly, many people choose complacency rather than becoming equipped to engage in the appropriate battles.

A patent we see often in the Bible is that God led people out "by the way of the wilderness."

In Exodus 13, after the Israelites had been delivered out of Egypt, God was very intentional about how He led them out.

Exodus 13:17 (ESV) says:

> God did not lead them by way of the land of the Philistines, although that was near. For God said, "Lest the people change their minds when they see war and return to Egypt."

So, He led them out by way of the wilderness toward the Red Sea, and they came up out of the land of Egypt equipped for battle.

What about the story of Jehoshaphat in 2 Chronicles 20 (NKJV)?

Jehoshaphat was a reformist known for operating in the fear of the Lord.

The Bible says that a great multitude of Moabites and Ammonites came against Jehoshaphat and his kingdom for battle. This was after his years of alliance with King Ahab. God had defeated his enemies in Israel, but this caused a rise of his enemies outside of Israel.

When Jehoshaphat learned of an approaching battle, he was afraid. However, his response was to "set his face" to seek the Lord, gather all the people of Judah, and proclaim a fast.

In the day of adversity, his strength was not small, and he completely depended on the favor of the Lord for this battle.

The Bible says that Jehoshaphat stood in the assembly and proclaimed in 2 Chronicles 20:5 (NKJV):

> O Lord God of our fathers, are You not God in heaven, and do You not rule over all the kingdoms of the nations, and in Your hand is there not power and might, so that no one is able to withstand You? Are You not our God, who drove out the inhabitants of this land before Your people Israel, and gave it to the descendants of Abraham Your friend forever? And they dwell in it, and have built You a sanctuary in it for Your name, saying, "If disaster comes upon us—sword, judgment, pestilence, or famine—we will stand before this temple and in Your presence [for Your name is in this temple], and cry out to You in our affliction, and You will hear and save."

He continues in verse 12:

> O our God, will You not judge them? For we have no power against this great multitude that is coming against us; nor do we know what to do, but our eyes are upon You.

Then, the Bible says that the Spirit of the Lord fell on Jahaziel, the son of Zechariah. He stood in the assembly and delivered the Word of the Lord in 2 Chronicles 20:15:

> Thus says the Lord to you: "Do not be afraid nor dismayed because of this great multitude, for the battle is not yours, but

God's. Tomorrow go down against them. They will surely come up by the Ascent of Ziz, and you will find them at the end of the brook before the Wilderness of Jeruel. You will not need to fight in this battle. Position yourselves, stand still and see the salvation of the Lord, who is with you, O Judah and Jerusalem!" Do not fear or be dismayed; tomorrow go out against them, for the Lord is with you.

Jehoshaphat and all of Judah bowed before the Lord and began to worship. The children of the Kohathites and Korahites stood up and began to praise the Lord loudly.

They rose early in the morning and went out into the Wilderness of Tekoa.

Again, Jehoshaphat stood and said in verse 20:

Hear me, O Judah and you inhabitants of Jerusalem: Believe in the Lord your God, and you shall be established; believe His prophets, and you shall prosper.

Then, he appointed those who could sing to the Lord, and they went out singing, "Praise the Lord, For His mercy endures forever."

As they began to sing and praise, the Lord set ambushes against their enemies and all who had come against Judah, and they were defeated.

Before Judah's armies even reached the battlefield, the Ammonites and Moabites attacked their own allies and destroyed them. Then, they destroyed each other.

Judah won the battle without even having to fight. The battle belonged to God. The only army the victory required was an army of worshipers who understood the awe and wonder of God's presence.

Jehoshaphat and the people of Judah reverenced His majesty more than the destructive forces of their enemies.

Jehoshaphat led through humility, trust, and a complete dependence on God. And he won the battle in the wilderness using spiritual weapons divinely powerful for the destruction of fortresses.

In Matthew 4 (NKJV), we see Jesus was led by the Holy Spirit into the wilderness after forty days of fasting to be a role model for how to approach the enemy.

The fasting and the wilderness season prepared Him to be tempted by the devil, submit to His Father, and resist the devil. The devil then fled from Him. He became the human template for how to overcome the temptation of the flesh in times of great pressure.

Jesus didn't avoid the wilderness, or the war, and He won the greatest war in history!

The wilderness season is meant to take you up, not keep you stuck. There are some battles that are assigned to you, but you may not be ready for them yet.

There are some battles that can only be won through preparation in the wilderness season, and God will not let you see them until you are fit for battle.

In hindsight, I know that if I didn't allow God to lead me and equip me through wilderness seasons, He would have given the battles He assigned me to someone else.

Think wisely and be intentional about your current or next wilderness season. Don't complain about the wilderness or become bitter in the wilderness.

There is a battle ahead that you are meant to lead and overcome from victory to victory.

What battles are you avoiding because you are afraid of what it may cost you? What areas do you put your faith in the enemy instead of your faith in God? Are you still stuck in a wilderness because you are not ready to surrender your self-dependence and trust that God is with you and will come through for you?

Prayer

Lord, I come to you today with my whole, undivided heart. You said you prepare a table for me in the presence of my enemies. I position my heart in surrender as I fix my gaze on you. You are a loving God, my fortress, my deliverer, and my shield in whom I take refuge. I praise you, Lord. You are my Rock. You train my hands for battle and my fingers for war. You alone give me strength for battle. With you as my strength, I can valiantly crush every enemy and advance through every stronghold that stands in front of me. Your goodness and mercy follow me all the days of my life. You give me the courage to continue to cut off the heads of giants and conquer every territory you give me. Teach me to fear you, Lord, and to walk in complete obedience. In Jesus' name, Amen.

Key Scriptures

Exodus 13:17 (ESV); 2 Chronicles 20:5–9, 12, 15, 17–22 (NKJV); Matthew 4 (NKJV)

Day 3

The Enemy Does Not Want to Steal Your Gift; He Wants to Steal The Oil That You Have Purchased in Secret.

The oil comes at a cost. Many people today live on borrowed oil and depend on others to carry their cross and fix their problems. The truth is that we are living in times where we must take responsibility to teach people how to purchase their own oil.

The parable of the ten virgins in Matthew 25:1-13 (TPT) explains this best. Jesus uses this parable to teach His disciples what the kingdom realm is like.

Jesus explained that the kingdom is like ten virgins who took their oil lamps to meet the bridegroom. Five of them were foolish because they were ill prepared, taking no extra oil for their lamps. On the other hand, the other five were wise because they took flasks of oil with their lamps. In other words, they were living in overflow because they had more than enough oil.

When the bridegroom was delayed, they all became drowsy and fell asleep but were suddenly awakened. The five virgins who had oil trimmed their lamps and were ready to encounter the bridegroom. Unfortunately, the five foolish virgins were running out of oil, so they begged the five wise virgins for oil. Because they were wise, the five wise virgins said, "We can't. We don't have enough for all of us. You'll have to go and buy some for yourselves!"

The five wise virgins were ready when the bridegroom came and were escorted inside. They enjoyed the wedding feast. Unfortunately, the five foolish virgins missed the arrival of the bridegroom. The door was locked, and they begged to come in, but the bridegroom responded in verse 12, "Do I know you? I can assure you, I don't even know you!"

Does this sound familiar? It sounds like Jesus' teaching on true and fake disciples in Matthew 7:21–23 (NIV):

> Not everyone who says to me, "Lord, Lord," will enter the kingdom of heaven, but only the one who does the will of my Father who is in heaven. Many will say to me on that day, "Lord, Lord, did we not prophesy in your name and in your name drive out demons and in your name perform many miracles?" Then I will tell them plainly, "I never knew you. Away from me, you evildoers!"

You can win the lost, heal the sick, and drive out demons in His name and not know Him intimately. You can check every Christianese box and fill every roster, but your oil will dry up and your wick will wither if you don't understand how to buy your own oil.

Jesus was illustrating that moving the heart of God is not about performance; it has everything to do with preference for proximity to Him. To prefer Him is to devote ourselves to Him, set our affections on Him, and to love Him not for what He has done but for who He is.

This comes at a cost. It will cost you your comfort, your time, and your plans. Many times, the oil comes in silence and stillness, or when He asks us to wait a little longer.

The Holy Spirit brings the oil, and He is like a dove looking for a place to land, but He won't land on moving targets. You must go beyond the distractions, the busyness, and the chaos into the oasis with God.

The oil must be purchased and protected. How do you protect the oil? Don't let a devil (even one in the form of a cell phone) or a seemingly Godly distraction in your secret place. Do not grieve the Holy Spirit through lack of repentance, and do not quench the Holy Spirit by cutting Him off or cutting Him short.

The oil is protected through humility, righteousness, and complete dependence.

Jesus modeled how to regularly build intimacy with the Father. Jesus knew how to purchase and protect His oil. The busier He became, the more He sought out solitude with God. He went lengths, and paid the price, to get that time. Many times, He rose very early or prayed through the night. Often, He went without food because nothing sustained or satisfied Him more than hearing His Father's voice.

Sometimes the crowds were buzzing around Him, but He still gave his Father preference. Jesus knew the authority that He carried to heal and cast out demons. He knew what He could do and what He should do. He would jump into a boat to go off to solitary places to get away from the crowds. Jesus didn't react to their situations; He responded to His Father.

After a time of seclusion and giving Himself to prayer, He emerged from His solitude to find crowds waiting for Him. The Bible says in Matthew 14:14 (TPT) that when He saw so many people, His heart, like His Father, was moved with compassion toward them, and He healed all who were sick.

He showed His disciples how to do the same, often leading them away from the chaos of the crowds into a quiet place.

It took the disciples awhile to understand the exchange that took place in their quiet times with Jesus, so Jesus had to show them. One example is in the feeding of the 5,000 in Matthew 14 (TPT).

When they tried to send the multitude away because they thought the provision was on them to feed the 5,000, Jesus responded, "They don't need to leave. You can give them something to eat."

The disciples didn't even realize that it was not about the five loaves and the two fish. It was not about their current provision, or lack thereof. It was *always* about how their proximity to Jesus gave them access to the provision.

To demonstrate this to them, Jesus had them look at Him. Then, He looked at His Father and gave thanks. He broke the bread, which symbolized giving Himself to them. As they received Him, they began distributing Him to the crowd. The miracle occurred when the disciples gave the crowd what they already had: Jesus. The provision multiplied, and they all ate until satisfied. They still filled twelve baskets of leftovers.

This is why the oil purchased in secret will always transcend human limitations. Are your gifts, performance, or man-made provisions going to help when you depend on a miracle? No, but what you have built in the secret place will.

You will have to maintain a gift that you operate in without anointing. I would rather depend on the resources of Heaven that are lubricated with oil than the resources of man that will eventually dry out and burn up.

Let's take time to take inventory of our secret place. Where have you been robbed by the enemy through distraction, busyness, and mixture? Where do you need the moisture from the Holy Spirit to lubricate your life again? Go into a quiet room, close the door, and pray this prayer.

Prayer

Holy Spirit, I invite you into my secret place today. Thank you for meeting me right where I am. I recognize that I have been pulled away by many distractions, but this privilege to come near you is essential over everything and everyone else in my life. I recognize my need for your nearness. Forgive me for operating in my own strength and neglecting the sacredness of our union. I quiet myself in your presence and allow your still, small voice to transcend my mind, will, and emotions. I sit with you and tune the ears of my heart to listen and obey. Wash me in your presence. Anoint my head with oil and let my cup overflow into the lives of others. Anoint me with the fragrance of the Holy Spirit and let it permeate every place the sole of my foot treads. I don't want anything outside of your presence. Your presence is my wraparound protection. Let everything in my life flow from this well. In Jesus' name, Amen.

Key Scriptures

Matthew 25:1–13 (TPT); Matthew 7:21–23 (NIV); Matthew 14:13–16, 20–21 (TPT)

Day 4

Fear Causes Us to Forfeit Our God-Given Identity and Take On The False Identity of Self-Preservation and Self-Sufficiency.

In Genesis 2 (NKJV), God plants the Garden of Eden. He puts Adam, the first man He made, in the garden to work it and keep it in order. Then, He creates Eve to be his helper and companion.

In Genesis 3 (NKJV), when the Garden of Eden is fully introduced, the garden is symbolic of our lives. Eden means "a place of pleasure and delight." The Garden of Eden had all the provisions that Adam and Eve needed. There was a wall of protection, which created an environment where the presence of God was tangibly felt. The Garden of Eden represented what the kingdom was like. It represented the role of God, our Father, as our provider and protector.

However, in this scenario, we also observe the intrusion of the devil. The Bible says he was skilled in deceit. He tried to elevate himself above God and got kicked out of Heaven. He was a created being who did not have a father, so he started a mission in the garden to make an orphan out of God's creation.

He found an opportunity where Adam was absent and Eve was vulnerable. He paints Eve a picture of the substitute, or "what she could have," to appeal to her flesh.

The devil contested the Word of God, asking her in Genesis 3:1, "Has God indeed said, 'You shall not eat of every tree of the garden?'"

In other words, "Eve, can you really trust God? Eve, you don't have to listen to God. Eat the fruit, and then you can become your own god." The devil's endgame was to turn Eve away from God and against herself.

Eve then influenced Adam. They perceived they lost their identity as God's children and took on the false identity of self-preservation and substitution. The Bible says the eyes of both of them were opened, and they knew that they were naked. They sewed fig leaves together, *made themselves* coverings, and began to protect themselves.

These man-made fig leaves were *fake* leaves that gave them a false sense of security. The fig coverings in this scenario represent shame. Because they identified themselves with shame, the Bible says that they became afraid. Consequently, they began to hide from God because they were afraid.

Instead of God being their Father and teacher, the substitutes of shame and fear became their teachers. Shame caused them to identify with what was wrong with them instead of what was right with them. They began to substitute their identity as God's children with the strongholds of fear and shame. As a result, they began to reject God's protection and began to live from the lie of substitution.

What happened to Adam and Eve, and what happens for many people, is they chose to lose their God-given protection and turn to self-preservation.

Anytime a person tries to protect themselves, they will eventually destroy themselves because they come out of alignment with God's design. Every replacement for God will eventually cause sickness and stress because our lives were meant to be a garden, not a grave. The counterfeit version will never give you life; it will always take life from you.

The devil's number-one fear is not what you will do on this Earth for Jesus. His number-one fear is your relationship and intimacy with God. He hated the intimacy that Adam and Eve had with God, so he perverted it, and is still on a mission to do so today.

He wants to use every substitute stronghold and distraction to rob you of intimacy. Lack of intimacy leads to prayerlessness. If he can get you not to talk to your Father, and if you can't hear your Father's voice, then you will never know the version of yourself that God knows. As a result, you will live the substitute version of the life God had designed for you.

Instead of having your own dream, you will live as a slave to someone else's dream.

The devil knows that intimacy precedes destiny. He knows that without intimacy, you will not fulfill the assignment that God has given you on Earth.

Later, in Genesis 3:8, the Lord came walking in the garden in the cool of the day. Adam and Eve were hiding, but God was searching. It wasn't that God didn't know where they were or that they had sinned, but He was trying to get them to locate themselves.

In Genesis 3:9, He calls to Adam, saying, "Where are you?"

So, they reveal to God that they were afraid and covered themselves.

But God didn't look at their behavior. He was more concerned about their hearts and belief systems, so He says in verse 11, "Who told you that you were naked?"

God gave them a chance to encounter truth, take responsibility for their sin, and restore their relationship. For God, the highest priority is always restoring us to the right relationship.

The Bible says that God wove together animal skins and clothed them to show them that they weren't responsible for their own coverings. He wanted to restore their identity as His children and take off the fake coverings of shame.

Although there were consequences for their disobedience, God wanted to show them that their behavior did not cause them to lose the covering and protection of a loving Father.

God is calling us back to the legitimacy of that moment. He is calling us back to the place that He originally intended us to be. We were never meant to provide for and protect ourselves, creating a false sense of security through self-preservation.

Are there areas of your life where you know you are not allowing God to be your true provider and protector? What areas have you wrapped yourself in the fake coverings of fear and shame to hide from God? What areas of your life have become the counterfeit substitutes to your God-given identity? Let us pray to restore and realign into the right relationship today.

Prayer

Lord, thank you for being a true Father who adopted me into a royal family and gave me the full rights of sonship. Forgive me for yielding to the spirit of fear and control, taking my life into my own hands, rejecting your provision and protection. Your Word says that I have not been given the spirit of bondage, leading me to fear of not being good enough, but I have received the spirit of adoption, the spirit that produces sonship. I am fully accepted and enfolded into the family of God. I renounce and break my agreement with fear, control, and shame. I take off these fake coverings that have led me into self-preservation and a life full of substitute gods. You are the one true God; every other god is counterfeit. I rise in my office and divine assignment and take authority over the atmosphere of my life. I receive the inheritance of every spiritual blessing in the heavenlies. In Jesus' name, Amen.

Key Scriptures

Genesis 2 (NKJV); Genesis 3:1–11 (NKJV)

Day 5

People Who Fear The Lord Praise; People Who Don't Complain.

Our words frame our worlds. Your world becomes the product of the words that you speak.

Proverbs 18:21 (NKJV) says, "Death and life are in the power of the tongue, And those who love it will eat its fruit."

I am pretty sure I like all fruit, but the one fruit I refuse to consume is dead fruit. Yet, many people consume it daily and wonder why their lives have a stench.

I got married in my late thirties after an extended season of being single. I wish I could say that I always managed that season well, but in various times of delay and disappointment, I rushed ahead of God and, sometimes, did not make the best decisions.

Instead of patiently trusting God to bring the right person into my life, many times, I foolishly tried to manufacture my own miracle.

When I became impatient, I turned to online dating apps. Let me clarify, online dating can be successful, but it is crucial to have good intentions and motives to avoid potential disasters and delays.

I was searching online for a Boaz, but I had not yet become the woman God needed me to become. There were a few instances where I went on dates with men who were not aligned with the future God had for me. While in most cases I didn't go on a second date, I shouldn't have entertained the first one.

And God, being a good Father, interrupted my little mission, saying, "Stop trying to manufacture your own miracle. Instead, participate in it with me because I am the perfect matchmaker."

God got my attention, and I did stop all the nonsense, but the words that I would speak still didn't line up.

I remember one time feeling so annoyed, disappointed, and hopeless about dating. Every time I thought about the world of dating, negative thoughts would come, followed by negative comments.

I exclaimed one day, "Men are just fearful cowards!"

I will never forget what happened next. I heard the voice of God, my Father, call me out. He said, "Dana, those aren't my men you are talking about. You are speaking from a filter of disappointment. Why don't you pray for them? Men carry a lot more than you think. If you keep sowing malice with your words, you are only going to produce more of what you are seeing right now."

God, being a good and loving Father, corrected me in love. I heeded that correction and asked for forgiveness, as I understood how my words had power to build up or destroy.

Even though I didn't always feel like it, I began to use my words to pray for them and encourage them despite what I saw in the natural.

God revealed to me how our words affect relationships in the context of scripture. This revelation applies to everyone: whether single, married, or in any relationship.

He had me read the story of Samson and Delilah to prove His point. He showed me that this wasn't the story of a famous haircut; it was the story of a nagging woman.

In summary, the story of Samson and Delilah can be found in the book of Judges 16 (NKJV). Samson was known for his great strength and long hair. The Philistines put Delilah up to finding out the source of Samson's strength so they could overtake him and give her a ransom.

Delilah yielded to the temptation and began to beg him for the secret to his strength. One version says that she nagged him nearly to death.

Samson finally broke down and succumbed to her nagging. He revealed the secret: that if a razor ever touched his head, he would instantly lose his strength.

As soon as the secret was revealed, Delilah alerted the Philistines. When Samson fell asleep, she cut off his braids, and immediately, his strength left him.

To make matters worse, Samson awoke to this cruel reality, and before he could even process what had occurred, the Philistine army came. They gouged out his eyes, shackled him, and put him into prison.

What a horrific story! God was able to take this story out of context and insert it into my situation to teach me something very valuable.

God spoke to me after I read this. He said, "Do you see what happened as a result of her nagging? First, his hair was cut off and he lost his strength. Then, his eyes were gouged out and he lost his vision. The outcome of all of this is that Samson lost his strength, lost his vision, and ended up in a prison bound in chains. This happens to so many men, Dana. The more women nag, the more men shrink."

When God called me out and revealed to me the rotten fruit my complaints were producing, it gave me the opportunity to break free from the bitter judgments and inner vows I had made to cope with the pain of my disappointments.

I took a season off from dating and sowed a whole year into prioritizing my relationship with God, finding complete fulfillment and security in Him.

Through that, my hope was restored, and I came back into alignment with God's Word and His plans. God brought me back to a place of complete trust in Him, not in my own self-dependence.

Many months later, I met my husband, Joel. Once that happened, I knew that God had put me through an extended process to make sure I had a solid foundation in Him because He wanted to set me up for success.

All the wisdom gained from lessons that I learned from my years of being single had to be implemented repeatedly in dating and now marriage.

Proverbs 12:4 (TPT) says:

> The integrity and strength of a virtuous wife transforms her husband into an honored king. But the wife who disgraces her husband weakens the strength of his identity.

Would I choose to be the virtuous wife that seeks to champion my husband, and would my dignity make him a king? Or would I dishonor him with my words, making them like a cancer to his inner man, strength, and identity?

Does he feel like a king who is strengthened when I speak to him? Or do I dent and tarnish his armor with my words?

He can become a king, or like Samson, become a slave to bondage. It is my virtue and my words that make the difference.

I have seen breakthrough after breakthrough in my relationship with myself, God, and others because I have learned to speak the words that God loves and not speak the words that He hates.

Our words will always affect us and others. The Bible says in Matthew 12:34–35 (TPT):

> For what has been stored up in your hearts will be heard in the overflow of your words! When virtue is stored within, the hearts of good, upright people will produce good fruit. But when evil is hidden within, those who are evil will produce evil fruit.

Where are your words locating you today? If your heart were to speak, would it say you bless people or curse people? When you open your mouth, do your words add value to people, including yourself, or rob them or yourself of value? Allow the Holy Spirit to help you take inventory today.

Prayer

Lord, I recognize that there are issues in my heart that are bleeding into my life. I surrender my disappointments, and I invite you, Holy Spirit, to come and recalibrate my heart today. Forgive me for the bitter words that I have spoken over myself and others. I cancel and withdraw all judgments I have made against myself and others. I renounce every agreement I have made with bitterness. Teach me again to fear you. Teach me again to love the way you love, forgive the way you forgive, and tremble in fear at the thought of grieving you. Let the words of my mouth and the meditation of my heart be acceptable in Your sight, O Lord, my strength, and my redeemer. Let my words be gracious, noble, just, pure, virtuous, and praiseworthy. In Jesus' name, Amen.

Key Scriptures

Proverbs 18:21 (NKJV); Judges 16 (NKJV); Proverbs 12:4 (TPT); Matthew 12:34–35 (TPT)

Section 6

Worship

Worship was not created for us; it was created for God. God doesn't need our worship, but we need to worship God because we become whatever we worship.

"For it was in Him that all things were created, in heaven and on earth, things seen and things unseen, whether thrones, dominions, rulers, or authorities; all things were created and exist through Him [by His service, intervention] and in and for Him."

Colossians 1:16, AMPC

True worshipers have an awe and fear of God. They know that how they approach Him determines what they will receive from Him.

True worshipers know that God keeps His eye on His friends, but His ears pick up every moan and groan.

True worshipers embrace peace and don't let it get away.

True worshipers turn their back on sin and do something good.

True worshipers guard their tongues against profanity, gossip, and lying.

When you are well educated in God's school of worship and make it your priority, as stated in Isaiah 45 (MSG), He promises to go ahead of you, clearing and paving the road. He'll break down bronze city gates, smash padlocks, kick down barred entrances, lead you to buried treasures, show you the secret caches of valuables, and give you confirmations.

He will give you the best of care if you'll only get to know and trust Him. True worship establishes and reinforces that there are no other real gods except God.

True worship opens the doors to all His goodness, and true worshipers have a zeal for life.

You can have anything when God is your everything.

This is not a religious statement, but rather a call to action that I believe God is urging us all to embrace. We ask Him to come down, but His desire is for us to come up.

I believe the level of your life is the level of your worship.

David became a king because he was a man after God's own heart.

Before he defeated Goliath, he built intimacy in the secret place as a shepherd in the field.

Before he went to war, he was found ministering to the Lord, which positioned him for victory.

Sometimes you will get stuck outside the gate if you don't know how to get access.

God is a king who deserves our welcome and our reverence.

This is the biggest key that has shifted my life. Whenever I have needed a breakthrough, there has been a "*wait-through.*"

Whenever I have seen an increase in power and anointing, it has been from seeking His face through worship.

When you receive access to the King and give Him a gift, He gives you everything He has.

God is looking to give Himself to *true* (sincere) worshipers, those who worship in spirit and in truth. Let us not leave anything on the table as we go into this next section, where you will learn that worship is not about singing the right song but positioning yourself to move the Father's heart.

Day 1

God Destroys Your Enemies to The Soundtrack of Your Praise.

What are you singing? What are you saying? What are you praying?

The enemy's number-one tactic is to unseat the soul and steal your song.

If he can steal your song through distraction, hardship, affliction, injustice, and weariness, he can steal your joy.

If he can steal your joy, he can steal your strength, your place of power, and prosperity.

Where there is no power and prosperity, there are victims and orphans who only influence themselves.

The Bible says in Psalms 100:4 (TPT) that praise is the passport that opens the gate; it is the way we enter.

Praise is not just a weapon; it is a gift.

When hell is all around you, the song of heaven is still within you. You can open your mouth and sing a song of praise to manifest heaven on Earth.

Sometimes, you must command your soul to praise until every kingdom bows its knee.

Isaiah 30:29 (AMP) says:

> You will have a song as in the night when a holy feast is kept, And joy of heart as when one marches [in procession] with a flute, To go to the [temple on the] mountain of the Lord, to the Rock of Israel.

Continuing in verse 32, it says:

> And every blow of the rod of punishment, Which the Lord will lay on them, Will be to the music of Israel's tambourines and lyres; And in battles, brandishing weapons, He will fight Assyria.

We all have seasons of warfare. If you haven't had one, it is coming.

There was a season of my life where there was very intense warfare. If it could go wrong, it did. There were obstacles in my finances, obstacles in my marriage, obstacles in my family, obstacles in my workplace, and obstacles in my ministry.

To say I felt hard-pressed on every side and perplexed was an understatement. I felt the Holy Spirit commission me to wait on the Lord and "war-ship."

As I waited on Him, I shifted my focus from my surroundings and set my affection on Him. I meditated on His goodness, faithfulness, longsuffering, might, and omnipotent power, and suddenly, His tangible presence filled the room.

I felt supernaturally strengthened in my inner man. I felt His might and power come upon me. I felt a surge of courage rise up. I worshiped to a place where I was no longer yearning for a change of my circumstances; I was yearning for Him. I was receiving Him and drinking from His well.

The Lord spoke to me. He said, "Remember, I am a warrior." As I leaned into this attribute in worship, I saw Him as my warrior, my protector and defender.

The longer I waited, worshiped, and went deeper into His presence, the more I could see Him fighting my battles.

Then he led me to Psalms 35:2–9 (TPT), where David cries out:

> Put on your armor, Lord; take up your shield and protect me. Rise up, mighty God! Grab your weapons of war and block the way of the wicked who come to fight me. Stand for me when they stand against me! Speak over my soul: "I am your strong Savior!" Humiliate those who seek my harm. Defeat them all! Frustrate their plans to defeat me and drive them back. Disgrace them all as they have devised their plans to disgrace me. Blow them away like dust in the wind, with the angel of Almighty God driving them back! Make the road in front of them nothing but slippery darkness, with the angel of YAHWEH behind them, chasing them away! For though I did nothing wrong to them, they set a trap for me, wanting me to fail and fall. Surprise them with your ambush, Lord, and catch them in the very trap they set for me. Let them be the ones to fail and fall into destruction! Then my fears will dissolve into limitless joy; my whole being will overflow with gladness because of your mighty deliverance.

I stayed in this posture for several days, and breakthrough after breakthrough came. All the circumstances that were meant to cause conflict came to nothing. This became my new default in worship. I worship until I can see Him.

Heaven loves the sound of our praise; we just need to tune into the frequency of Heaven. Heaven has one sound, and if you learn to tap into it, you will see and experience the glory, authority, power, weight, magnitude, and wisdom of our mighty God.

Prayer

Heavenly Father, I come before you and set my affection on you. You are a King that deserves my highest praise and reverence. I was created by you and for you, and in you, I have my whole being. I was created for the purpose of worshiping you. You are unrivaled, unlimited, and unmatched in beauty. When you speak, the mountains shake, the Earth quakes, and the darkness trembles. Let God arise and let every enemy scatter. Show up in glory, show up in power, show up in majesty. Drench me with your presence. Anoint me with the fragrance of the Holy Spirit. In Jesus' name, Amen.

Key Scriptures

Psalm 100:4 (TPT); Isaiah 30:29, 32 (AMP); Psalms 35:2–9 (TPT)

Day 2

The Only Wilderness You Stay in is The One You Complain in; Make The Choice to Rejoice.

It's time to exchange the "woe is me" for victory.

I remember many years ago, I was struggling financially. This was an area that I never struggled in, but I was going through an unexplained season.

A beautiful woman of God who I call Mama Kwacha became very concerned about me, so she prayed in her midnight prayers and asked the Holy Spirit what it was. Then, she sent me several messages where the theme was praise.

She said, "Your money is not your problem."

Upon reflection, I realized that I had spent too much time complaining about the unfairness of life. I had not processed some of the circumstances that had happened in my life that were beyond my control. Due to repressed emotions and unprocessed grief, a bitter root rose up and began to manifest.

I was meant to walk through the valley of Baca to become a wellspring of life for others, but unfortunately, I was staying in the wilderness of Mara, the place of bitterness.

I began to turn my complaints into praise. In a very short time, I walked right out of that wilderness, and now can impact many more people in this area.

The Bible says in Ecclesiastes 3:1 (NLT) that there is a time and season for everything. There is a time for mourning and sorrow, but then there is a time to exchange the garment of heaviness for the garment of praise, and not allow a season to turn into a lifestyle.

The story of David illustrates this in 2 Samuel 12 (ESV).

After David had an affair with Bathsheba and had her husband, Uriah, killed, Bathsheba became pregnant and bore a child who was afflicted with sickness.

David fasted, prayed, and sought God on behalf of the child. On the seventh day of his fasting, the child died.

When David's advisors came to report the news to him, they expected him not to listen, even to do harm to himself, but that was not David's response.

He got up, removed his sackcloth, took a bath, and went to the House of the Lord to worship. Then, he came home and ate because even though he couldn't change the circumstance or bring his son back, he could live in hope that he would see him again. As a result, he was able to rise up to be a rock and comfort Bathsheba during this time.

David worshiped in the wilderness of tragedy, and that season produced Solomon—one of the wealthiest, wisest, and most powerful men in the Bible. Like his father, he was a man after God's own heart who showed God deep reverence and worship. This would never have been possible if David had stayed wrapped in his sackcloth and grief.

There is a time to rise out of grief and sorrow and move toward recovery.

Jesus, Himself, was acquainted with sorrow because He faced the ultimate rejection of men, yet He didn't become a victim. He bore our sorrows and took them upon Himself so that by His stripes, we can be healed.

Isaiah 61:3 (NKJV) paints the perfect picture of the beautiful exchange Jesus made for us at Calvary:

> To console those who mourn in Zion, To give them beauty for ashes, The oil of joy for mourning, The garment of praise for the spirit of heaviness; That they may be called trees of righteousness, The planting of the Lord, that he may be glorified.

What circumstance are you facing that you know you need to put the sackcloth to rest and put on a garment of praise? What language of complaint do you need to change to experience God's promises and prosperity for your life?

We are not victims; we are co-heirs with Christ. Make the choice to stay in faith, in a posture of worship, and see Him move miraculously on your behalf.

Prayer

Lord, I come to you and ask you to examine my heart. I repent for complaining and for elevating my words above your words. I renounce every agreement I have made with bitterness. I withdraw and revoke every single word curse and bitter judgment I have spoken against myself and others. I choose to take off my sackcloth, lay it at the cross, and pick up a garment of praise. I will praise you, Lord. You have heard my cry. You have brought me up out of the pit and the miry clay. You have set my feet upon a rock and established my steps. You have put a new song in my mouth. Praise to our God! In Jesus' name, Amen.

Key Scriptures

Ecclesiastes 3:1 (NLT); 2 Samuel 12:15–20 (ESV); Isaiah 61:3 (NKJV)

Day 3

If You Want a New Season, You Need to Sing a New Song.

In the journey of life, we go through many significant seasons. One of the seasons that changed the trajectory of my life was when God taught me to sing a new song.

I used to think it was an old wives' tale for women to truly experience the biological "ticking clock." I used to think the idea of a magical number was silly, a way for women to justify their emotions and fill a void.

When I reached my mid thirties, I suddenly felt a heaviness, as the reality that I had not yet become a mother hit me for the first time. Being a mother was always my first calling, so going through this circumstance was unexpected.

The devil used my grievous, vulnerable state to weave a partial truth into my mind and convinced me to accept it.

One day, amid my grief, I heard him whisper, "Dana, maybe you should think about starting to let go of the idea of having a family. Perhaps, you need to accept this different plan for your life and begin the process of moving forward. After all, you are in your mid thirties. By the time you find someone, settle down, and have a family, you will be past the age of having children."

My heart began to immediately buy this lie. I thought, *You know what, that is probably true. Perhaps, the enemy is right.*

A spirit of sorrow and grief entered my heart as the tears began to fall. I remember crying myself to sleep for many nights during that time.

To make things even worse, coincidentally, I was at work with all my "me too" friends, aka my coworkers.

They began to ask me crazy questions like, "Have you ever thought about donating your eggs since you are already in your mid thirties?" "Have you ever thought about being a surrogate mother and blessing someone else since it isn't really working out for you?"

The one that really put me over the top was when a nurse even asked me, "Would you consider artificial insemination since you still want children but aren't yet married?"

You cannot make this stuff up.

It all seems absurd to admit that the enemy was right or to entertain the fear-based questions from my coworkers. In my normal state of faith, the enemy would not even get a foothold, but in the state I was in, it became a reality, and the deep pangs of grief and sorrow grew more intense on the inside. I literally felt like my heart was going to break. It felt like a part of me had just died.

The more I entertained thoughts of hopelessness, grief, and tears, the more I found comfort in them.

Those comforts began to feel good. If I grieved and cried long enough, I could numb the pain and fear that encompassed my devastation.

In hindsight, that pain had been in place for some time. Since I was a child, I had always loved and enjoyed children. The first call of God that I knew was on my life was to be a mother. I realized that I had distanced myself from children. I had not held a baby in a long time because it was a reminder of a promise unfulfilled. My avoidance was my coping mechanism to protect myself from pain.

During this time, I spent a long time struggling with grief and despair, until our women's ministry held a night where women were set free from grief, fear, and unbelief.

I did get a high level of breakthrough during that meeting, but God continued the work that night before I went to sleep.

I crawled in my bed, opened my Bible, and my eyes fell onto a scripture that would take the breakthrough to the next level. It was a scripture that God told me to sing repeatedly to replace the devastation. This scripture would now become the new default for hope in His promises.

The scripture was Psalms 113:9 (NLT), which says, "He gives the childless woman a family, making her a happy mother. Praise the Lord!"

His Word pierced my heart deeply. The Lord ministered to me and confirmed His promises. As I encountered God, He told me to "begin to sing what I wanted to see."

I began to put that into practice. In a short period of time, an unexplainable measure of hope filled me on the inside as I sang this new song. I couldn't get it out of my spirit. The devastation, loss, and grief from the weeks before had passed.

What I learned was that the enemy will always try to lead you toward self-destruction. He will get you to claim *barren* in whatever area of your life you feel you are not producing fruit and attempt to stamp you with the mark of hopelessness. If he can entice you to come into agreement, his job is done, so he moves on. You will need to break that agreement and sing a new song to get back up.

See, as Christians, we need to recognize we are co-heirs with Christ. Maybe we would not spend so much time begging God in the prayer closet if we could use the authority we have been given to turn those prayers into songs of praise for what has already been given.

I loved the newfound hope and dream that God had put inside my heart. I began to put my thoughts toward this dream. I began to sing over my future family. As I sang this new song, I canceled every word curse spoken over my future family. I called them blessed and still release this over them every day.

The new song of hope I was singing over my life became my new default and reality. I had such a revelation of the truth of His word that burned inside of me that the circumstances around my "me too" coworkers' conversations seemed illegitimate and irrational.

If we want a new season, we must sing a new song. We cannot expect God to change our season if we will not change our song.

We wouldn't have a "me too" generation wrecked by victim mentality if we had more people singing "but God" songs.

What are the areas in your life where you have made agreements with the devil's lies and become prey to his deceptive tactics? What are the areas you have become sick in your soul from yielding to the lies of the devil instead of the truth of God's promises? Let us sing a new song of faith today as we pray from scripture into the breakthrough today.

Prayer

Lord, I come to this altar today to surrender every lie and renounce every agreement I have made with unbelief, fear, control, and grief. As I sing a new song, my praise will command every distressing spirit to leave my life. I lift a great shout of praise and sing my way into your presence with joy. According to Psalm 100:4 (TPT), I pass through your open gates with the password of praise. I bring you my offering of thanks and come right into your presence. I affectionately bless your beautiful name. As I sing this new song, I see my hope restored. I see my new season. I see your promises fulfilled, and I attach my amen to every word that you have sent over my life. I sing of your goodness and your faithfulness. I testify of your miracles, your mighty power and wonder. I am breaking through the stronghold of defeat, and I see myself standing at the finish line of victory. In Jesus' name, Amen.

Key Scriptures

Psalm 113:9 (NLT); Psalm 100:4 (TPT)

Day 4

Before You Bring God Your List, Bring Him a Gift.

The way you approach God is how you will receive from Him. The outcome of your intimacy with God changes when you have a revelation that He is the answer and the reward.

John 4:23–24 (TPT) says:

> From now on, worshiping the Father will not be a matter of the right place but with a right heart. For God is a Spirit, and he longs to have sincere worshipers who adore him in the realm of the Spirit and in truth.

Worshipers never approach God as if He is a genie in a bottle because they have a revelation of His holiness. They don't wait outside of His presence with their lists of requests because they understand that when you seek His face, you will see His provision.

Worshipers never have to wonder what encountering His presence looks like. Their worship is a response to the revealed Word of God.

Worshipers devote themselves to His Word because His Word reveals His attributes. His Word reveals what He desires, what He loves, and what pleases Him.

Worshipers understand that the point of worship is to exalt God exclusively, not ourselves.

Proverbs 25:6–7 (NKJV) says:

> Do not exalt yourself in the presence of the king, And do not stand in the place of the great; For it is better that he say to you, "Come up here," Than that you should be put lower in the presence of the prince, Whom your eyes have seen.

Worshipers never approach God casually. They recognize that He is a King. When you approach a King with a gift, you move His heart.

There is a reason the story of the woman with the alabaster jar is in all four gospels. In three of the four gospels, Jesus prophesied that this woman would be remembered wherever the gospel was spread because of her act of sacrifice and lavish devotion to Him. Whenever something is mentioned in all four gospels, we should pay attention.

In Mark's account of this story in Mark 14 (TPT), the Bible says Jesus was at the home of Simon, whom Jesus had healed of leprosy. As He was seated at the table, a woman with an alabaster flask filled with the highest quality of fragrant and expensive oil approached Him. She broke open the flask and poured the oil over His head. Mark describes it as "an extreme gesture of devotion."

When the witnesses saw this, they became angry because they thought she was wasting what could have been sold for a large amount of money, and they scolded her.

Jesus said to them in verse 6:

> Leave her alone! Why are you so critical of this woman? She has honored me with this beautiful act of kindness. You will always have the poor, whom you can help whenever you want, but you will not always have me. When she poured the fragrant oil over

me, she was preparing my body in advance of my burial. She has done all that she could to honor me. I promise you that as this wonderful gospel spreads all over the world, the story of her lavish devotion to me will be mentioned in memory of her.

This story is one of the most symbolic depictions of what worship does to move the Father's heart. When we bring him a gift through a sacrifice of worship, it is costly. The alabaster flask itself was considered a luxury. This fragrant and expensive oil was believed to cost 300 denarii, or about a year's wages for the average worker.

According to John's gospel, it was about twelve ounces, so it would have dripped from Jesus' head down to His garments and feet. Some scholars believe that when the Roman soldiers pierced Jesus' feet and placed the crown of thorns on His head, He could have still smelled of this fragrant oil.

This woman came to bring Jesus what was most precious to her and met Him in a face-to-face encounter. She didn't come to Him with her requests or even to praise Him for what He had done for her; she only wanted to minister to Him and touch Him. God had given His most precious to her; she was now giving what was most precious to her back to Him.

As that precious and fragrant oil dripped down Jesus' garments, this woman was in a position for that oil to drip on her. She came to anoint Him, but she left smelling like Him.

When we bring an offering in worship, and the Lord catches the fragrance of that sacrifice, He releases the anointing. We leave the altar smelling like Him, releasing that into the atmosphere of every place we walk into.

True worshipers continually give back to God what He has given them. They bring their offering to Him with a burning heart and continue to throw more wood on that flame.

When you move the Father's heart through adoration and extravagant worship, and the anointing comes, you can ask for anything, and you will receive it.

You don't have to labor in prayer to get answers when you labor in love.

I have found that my deepest worship has come in times of deep pain. It is when I love and adore Him even when I am tired, weary, frustrated, or disappointed.

It is much more costly when it is not convenient. It is much more costly to give away the comfort that I want to hold on to, but once I begin to adore Him, an exchange takes place.

When I exchange my comfort or my pain for His presence, the reward is Jesus. When we receive Jesus, we receive His joy, compassion, kindness, generosity, power, and resurrection.

When I minister to others, I see bodies healed and people set free from oppression because they don't encounter me; they encounter Jesus.

Have you found that you have lost your awe and wonder of God, treating Him as common instead of Holy? Has Jesus been treated like a second-class citizen in His own kingdom instead of the King? Has he become an addition to your schedule instead of the CEO of your life? Let us pray to shift the posture of our hearts today. Be restored back to the heart of worship for our Father.

Prayer

Lord Jesus, I lift my eyes up to gaze at you. You are a King that deserves my highest honor and reverence. You are Holy, and I approach your throne today to exalt You and You alone. You are exalted to the highest position and authority in the heavenly realm. Be enthroned for the glory of your name. I am in awe of your beauty, your splendor, and your majesty. I am in awe of your unfailing love, your faithfulness and goodness. My heart burns for your nearness. I am here simply to show my affection and love for you. I worship you and empty myself out, taking the seat of a servant. Inhabit my worship and fill me with you so that I may spill you on to others. In Jesus' mighty and matchless name, Amen.

Key Scriptures

John 4:23-24 (TPT); Proverbs 25:6–7 (NKJV); Mark 14:6–9 (TPT)

Day 5

You Can Praise God For What He Has Done, But Worship is When You See Him Face-to-Face.

One of the most extraordinary encounters I have experienced in worship was at a Jesus Image pastors conference in Orlando, Florida.

My husband and I had been through a season of much testing, trials and desperately needed to separate ourselves and be refreshed.

We didn't attend for God to deliver us out of our circumstances; we went with no other agenda than to meet Jesus face-to-face.

The room was electric, filled with people who were hungry for the power and presence of God. The atmosphere was pregnant with expectation for the King to come, and I could sense the tangible reverence and awe that the people had for Jesus.

I will never forget the sound of the first chord on the piano and the ambiance of the keys sustaining the same note, filling the room.

I will never forget the clarity of the atmosphere as if there was no earthly mixture. Even with my eyes closed, I had a sense everyone in the room had their eyes fixed on Jesus.

As everyone began to sing songs of love and adoration to Jesus, singing spontaneously in the spirit, I began to sense swells and swells of symbols, strings, voices, and harmonies. I could feel a tangible wind blow into the room. I had been swept up into the throne room with Jesus, and He began to impart rhema words to me. I could see a clear vision of my life.

At the climax of worship, I saw a vision of Jesus entering the room welcomed by the Holy procession. He was riding in on a white horse to inhabit the praises of His people. I had never felt so much weight in worship as the glory came and filled the whole room.

When Jesus entered the room, I opened my eyes for a moment just to see that none of the worship team was facing the audience. There was a wooden cross in the center of the stage. They were all facing the cross and ministering to the Lord.

The worship leader put his instrument down and fell on his face, worshiping, and ministering to the Lord. In most meetings, this would have thrown people off, but not in this meeting. The people did not depend on the worship leader. They were not looking at him because they were looking at the Lord.

Miracles began to break out as people were getting healed in their bodies and delivered from oppression. I felt the grief and pain I had brought with me leave completely. My husband, who had not been able to sleep well for ten years, was instantly delivered and healed. Not a single person laid hands on us, but it was the anointing that came and broke the yolk.

Revelation 7:9–17 (TPT) paints a picture of what happens when we minister to the Lord and reminds us that Heaven will resound our worship and back us up:

> After this I looked, and behold, right in front of me I saw a vast multitude of people—an enormous multitude so huge that no one could count—made up of victorious ones from every nation, tribe, people group, and language. They were all in glistening white robes, standing before the throne and before the Lamb with palm branches in their hands. And they shouted out

with a passionate voice: "Salvation belongs to our God seated on the throne and to the Lamb!" All the angels were standing in a circle around the throne with the elders and the four living creatures, and they all fell on their faces before the throne and worshiped God, singing: "Amen! Praise and glory, wisdom and thanksgiving, honor, power, and might belong to our God forever and ever! Amen!" Then one of the elders asked me, "Who are these in glistening white robes, and where have they come from?" I answered, "My Lord—you must know." Then he said to me, "They are ones who have washed their robes and made them white in the blood of the Lamb and have emerged from the midst of great pressure and ordeal. For this reason they are before the throne of God, ministering to him as priests day and night, within his cloud-filled sanctuary. And the enthroned One spreads over them his tabernacle-shelter. Their souls will be completely satisfied. And neither the sun nor any scorching heat will affect them. For the Lamb at the center of the throne continuously shepherds them unto life —guiding them to the everlasting fountains of the water of life. And God will wipe from their eyes every last tear!

Ministering to the Lord is the greatest weapon of warfare you can pick up.

The palm tree in this scripture symbolizes victory, which is the position we take in worship. When we can see Him seated on the throne, we can see Him seated higher than any circumstance.

The white robes represent our cleansing from the stain and defilement of the world now made white with the blood of the Lamb. Because of that blood, we no longer have to go to a priest, who has to atone for our sins; Jesus' resurrection made atonement for us. The priest no longer has to enter the tabernacle because our body has now become the temple that He can inhabit, dwell, and make His residence with us.

The emerging from major oppression, persecution, and tribulation represents the resurrection power that has been given so that believers can continuously overcome and go deeper into the realm of the kingdom.

When your soul is completely satisfied, it is because you have tasted Jesus. He completely fills us with His love so we never have to hunger and thirst for the temporal pleasures of the world.

No sun or scorching heat will affect us, means that no demonic power can afflict us when His presence dwells in us. Every demon must bow its knee to the name of Jesus.

His presence brings living springs of water to refresh us and anoints every tear shed from our eyes.

The Lord is always looking for a vessel to fill. When we minister to Him, we become an empty container that He can fill.

When you become a carrier of the presence, you refresh and bring life to everything around you. You can face any trial, tribulation, or persecution because you have a position of victory. Carriers of His presence bring resurrection to dead things.

This doesn't have to be a corporate meeting. You can go to a quiet room, close the door, turn on instrumental worship music, and have a supernatural encounter with the Lord.

Ministering to the Lord in worship is not a song you sing; it is a posture of a burning heart. At any time, if you are willing to fix your eyes on Him and linger, you can have this experience too.

Prayer

I lift my hands and my face to you, Lord. Holy, Holy, Holy is your name. You are worthy to receive all the glory, the honor, and the praise.

Who is like you, Lord? Where could I find anyone as glorious as you? Nothing can compare to your matchless beauty. At the mighty display of your Glory, every enemy must scatter, every stormy wave must be still, every stronghold must be crushed. Breathtaking and awesome is your power! Astounding and unbelievable is your might and strength on display. I long to walk in the radiance of your presence. You are our King, the holiest of all. Your wraparound presence is my protection. In Jesus' name, Amen.

Key Scriptures

Revelation 7:9–17 (TPT)

Conclusion

Esther is one of my favorite women in the Bible. Although God's name is not mentioned in the book of Esther, His footprints are everywhere throughout her life.

Esther was one of the greatest heroes of the faith, a woman who laid down her life to save her people from death. She was a prophetic picture of Jesus.

Esther's Hebrew name was "Hadassah," which means myrtle. The myrtle tree was a symbol of kingdom prosperity.

Isaiah 55:13 (NKJV) is a promise from God that mentions the significance of the myrtle tree:

> Instead of the thorn shall come up the cypress tree, And instead of the brier shall come up the myrtle tree; And it shall be to the Lord for a name, For an everlasting sign that shall not be cut off.

The brier represents death and drought, but the myrtle represents a long-lasting, fragrant tree of healing.

The myrtle tree has strong root systems that, even when cut down to the stump, sprout back stronger, able to withstand any harsh climate or condition.

Myrtle trees grow slowly, and the struggle and stress during their growth process causes them to have unique patterns. When seen on a hill or in a pasture, the mature myrtle appears so symmetrical that it seems to be a meticulously pruned, cultivated tree.

I have always wanted to model my life after Esther, and I have gone through many harsh, difficult things, but God has never let me keep my briers. He has slowly developed me and increased my capacity through pain and challenges, which has *always* led to blessings.

It is the secret place where God has made me into that myrtle tree. He has made me a tree of healing, a tree of prosperity, a tree that, though it has been cut down to the stump many times, always rises and grows back stronger.

In this world, we will all have the temptation to stay in control, but I encourage you to let go. Do not keep your briers.

Let God be the surgeon that prunes you. Let His Word be like a scalpel that pierces you to heal you. Whenever God filets you open, there is always a promise given, allowing you to rise like I have and like our friend, "Hadassah", Esther, did.

It is not how you get cut down, but it is how you grow back. It is always to bring generational prosperity and healing.

Let that be your motivation. Let every challenge that life brings be an opportunity to allow your roots to go deeper. Your secret place is the sacred place that creates that space.

Made in the USA
Las Vegas, NV
13 April 2025